THE SHIFTING SANDS
OF
CAM RANH BAY
R.V.N.
1965 - 1972

THE SHIFTING SANDS
OF
CAM RANH BAY
R.V.N.
1965 - 1972

A TRUE STORY
OF THE U.S.A.F. COMBAT NURSES
TOLD BY LT. COL. CAROLYN J. EBERHART
U.S.A.F. NC. RET.

WRITTEN BY JANICE STROUD SENTIF

THE SHIFTING SANDS OF CAM RANH BAY R.V.N.
1965-1972 – A True Story Of The U.S. Air Force Combat Nurses
© 2012 by Janice Stroud Sentif and Lt. Col. Carolyn J. Eberhart
U.S.A.F. NC. Ret. All rights reserved.

Published by: Lt. Col. Carolyn J. Eberhart U.S.A.F. NC. Ret.
WWW.SHIFTINGSANDSOFCAMRANHBAY.COM
Written by: Janice Stroud Sentif

ISBN: 978-0-615-60804-4

LOC#: TXu 1-789-474

Cover Design, Book Formatting and Layout by:
Eli Blyden | www.CrunchTimeGraphics.NET

Printed in the United States of America by:

Category: Non-Fiction, Historical, Biographical, Vietnam, Cam Ranh Bay, Military, Combat Nurses

DEDICATION

This book is dedicated to all the people who served on the Cam Ranh Peninsula… those that came home and those that did not.

FOR THOSE WHO HAVE FOUGHT FOR IT,
FREEDOM HAS A TASTE THE PROTECTED WILL
NEVER KNOW…

–Author Unknown

CONTENTS

PREFACE

I was stationed at Myrtle Beach, South Carolina, when I received my Orders assigning me to Cam Ranh Bay in Vietnam. I arrived at the Station on the second day of November, 1969. During my orientation, I realized what a large Air Base it was. We had all services assigned there, Army, Navy, Marines, Air Force and civilians. Most of the people arrived in three areas of Vietnam: Saigon, Cam Ranh Bay and Da Nang.

From August 1964 to May 7, 1975, we had 2,709,918 Americans in uniform in Vietnam. Only about 7,500 women served in Vietnam.

I want to tell the true story of the Air Force Hospital and let the world know of the wonderful work done by the doctors, nurses and last but not least, the corpsmen.

One way to do this is to tell of my experiences and those of the other nurses that were there.

When we were under emergency attack, no one wanted to be alone. People would crawl down the hall and ask if they could join you. In a few minutes, you would have five or six nurses in flack jackets and helmets just talking and trying not to be afraid.

It was extremely difficult, day after day, seeing and treating these very young soldiers. They were severely wounded.

The base was like a peninsula and you couldn't go anywhere. You felt like you were in prison. Our only recreation was to get a truck and go to the beach which was five miles away.

A lot of my friends that served with me in Vietnam are now deceased.

It is to honor them and their services that I write this true story.

INTRODUCTION

This is the true story of the nurses who served a twelve month tour of duty with the 12th/483rd USAF Hospital, Cam Ranh Bay Air Base, Republic of Vietnam from 1965-1972. It was a nasty war in a remote land on the far side of the world; its rationale a mystery to many who were called to sacrifice for a country not fully committed to the fray. This is an untold story of the second largest military hospital in South Vietnam and of its courageous medical team. It is a poignant tale of the countless wounded soldiers whose mangled bodies were pieced together and often sent back into the endless battle.

After the dedication of the Vietnam Women's Memorial and the Nurse's March on November 11, 1993, I found myself dismayed at the lack of publicized accurate information regarding the history, mission and success of the second largest Air Force Hospital. After communicating with other nurses who served there and with their immeasurable aid and support, I decided, to the best of my ability, to chronicle the history of the base from it's inception to closure. The hospital provided medical treatment to military of all branches of service and anyone who served regardless of nationality as well as civilians.

The services provided by the 485 bed hospital included General Surgery, Chest Surgery, Neurosurgery, Orthopedics, Urology, Ophthalmology, Dental Surgery, Preventive Medicine, Public Health Medicine, Medical Civic Action Programs and a 200 bed capacity Casualty Staging Unit.

I would like to give special recognition to the U.S. Army Nurses who provided services that played a major role in the day to day operation of the Cam Ranh Bay Air Base.

Time has blurred my memories through a filter of retrospection, colored by personal experiences, and age has if I have erred by omission or inclusion, it is because of human fallibility and the unique impact that war has on individuals.

MY ORDERS HAVE ARRIVED

Along with the arrival of my orders to report to Cam Ranh Bay Air Force Base in Vietnam, came the big questions: Where is it located? How do I get there? Why is the United States Military there?

My orders arrived in August 1969, and I had many questions concerning the assignment, and this country's role in the war. The next morning the Myrtle Beach Newspaper had the headlines "Hospital at Cam Ranh Bay Hit by VC!"

I quickly located some military personnel that had been stationed in Vietnam and asked them what to expect. They gave me a little background on the location and history. With further research, I found that the Vietnam civilization predated Christianity. In 20 B.C., a renegade Chinese General established a capital in the North and proclaimed himself emperor of "Nam Viet." It's History recorded centuries of resistance by the Independent and Nationalist Vietnamese, first to the Chinese, then French, Japanese, and again to the French.

The Vietnamese defeated the French at the Battle of Dien Bien Phu. The Geneva Accord agreement of 1954 set a demarcation line at the 17th parallel dividing Vietnam into North and South Vietnam.

Processing for incoming Military was usually carried out at Saigon, Cam Ranh and Da Nang.

My orders stated I would depart the U.S. from McCord AFB, Washington. There would be stops at Anchorage, Alaska, and Japan for refueling.

THIS WAS OUR LETTER OF ASSIGNMENT TO CAM RANH BAY, VIETNAM:

Reference is made to your assignment to the 12th USAF Hospital, Cam Ranh Bay, Vietnam. Since the supply channels are not yet well established and you will be pioneering for the first few months, the following uniform items are required for female nurses:

1. All mandatory uniform items, summer and winter

2. Slacks, poly, woman's, series 8415-minimum three pair

3. Shirt, woman's cotton, series 8415-minimum three

4. Boots, combat, man's black-one pair

5. Socks, man's, wool, cushion sole, black-four pair

6. Shoes, oxford, black-two pair

7. Anklets, wool or cotton, blue-four pair

8. White hospital duty uniform-eight each

9. White hospital duty cap with braid, two each

10. Shoes, oxford, white-two pair

11. The following items are recommended:

12. Civilian raincoat, plastic

13. T-shirts

14. Overshoes

15. Civilian clothes to include a cocktail dress and summer cottons

16. Sanitary supplies, three to four months supply

17. Towels and wash clothes

Due to the semi-tropical climate Vietnam, mildew is prevalent. You are cautioned against taking any items that cannot withstand the climate. Baggage allowance as stated in AFM-40, par. 55062(c) is: accompanied baggage, sixty pounds; unaccompanied baggage, six hundred pounds.

Lt. Colonel Ellen Respini, Flight Nursing Branch, Brooks Air Force Base, Texas has been selected as your chief nurse. (She was the first chief nurse and others followed.)

Should you have any difficulties in obtaining the required uniform items, or need assistance in any way please contact me at extension 3595 or 3596, Rudolph AFB, Texas.

Sincerely,
Bernadette F. Calnon, Lt. Colonel, USAF, NC
Medical Career Division Office of the Assistant Surgeon General for Staffing and Education

WALKING THE FLOOR TO NAM!!!

We had to report several hours before the plane was to depart for Vietnam. Most people "Walked the Floor" in anticipation, and many remarks like "This is as close to Canada as we're going to get" were heard. People waited in line to use the telephone, just one more phone call to a loved one. Everyone was a bundle of nerves.

We departed the United States on 02 November, 1969, aboard a civilian chartered plane. There were 219 passengers, and Col. Ladner and I were the only female passengers on board.

It became very cold on the plane. Luckily I had brought my military coat with the lining. Col. Ladner had a small cosmetic bag which she used to put her feet on…We fought over that coat–blanket, and the cosmetic bag, our foot stool, all the way to Vietnam.

It was a long journey from McCord AFB to Anchorage and on to Japan. We refueled in Japan. They had armed guards meeting the plane in Japan just in case anyone had any idea of going AWOL. We stopped for a few hours; this gave us the opportunity to shop for items we may have forgotten to bring with us. When they called the flight for boarding, we were "marched" to the plane between the armed guards.

Food was plentiful and it seemed like they were forever serving meals on the flight. Everyone was very quiet and dejected despite the food.

When the plane approached Cam Ranh Bay Airbase, they turned off the interior lights. After the plane landed, a GI in fatigues boarded. When the airplane door was opened, the intense heat and humidity really hit you. Goldie (Col. Ladner) said: "You can have your coat back"! Well, little did I know my coat would be borrowed about five times by various nurses going back to "The World" on PCS[1]...that coat was always faithfully dry cleaned and returned to me, ready for the day "My Freedom Bird" would arrive. Oh, by the way Goldie, "You can have your cosmetic bag, our foot stool back!!!"

---

[1]Permanent change of station.

CAM RANH CADILLAC

Not knowing I would get orders to go to Vietnam, I had recently purchased a new car. Rather than store it for a year, I loaned it to my sister for the year I would be gone. The first realization that I was "without wheels" came when I needed a ride to the airport!

When we arrived in Vietnam, the Chief Nurse met us. She had one of the corpsmen drive the ambulance. The next morning we were told to go process in and get our combat gear. Combat gear consisted of a duffle bag full of things like; flak jacket, helmet, gas mask, fatigues, and combat boots, etc. That bag was REALLY heavy. We started out carrying it back to our quarters. Along the way someone saw us and felt sorry for us and gave us a ride in a jeep.

After looking over the situation, I realized our mode of transportation for the next year would be deuce & ½ trucks, jeeps, ambulances, feet and friends unless I made some other arrangements.

Several months later, I had friends purchase a bicycle in Hong Kong and ship it to Cam Ranh Bay. That bicycle became my CAM RANH CADILLAC. I could transport both a care package and a case of beer tied on the back!

When I left Cam Ranh I gave my bicycle to the Head Nurse of the 26th CSU. Lt. Col Gerri Deptula in turn bestowed the Cam Ranh Cadillac on the new Chief Nurse. I've often wondered what ever happened to my beautiful, wine colored Cam Ranh Cadillac.

Carolyn J. Eberhart on Cam Ranh Cadillac

14TH AERIAL PORT SQUADRON CAM RANH BASE TERMINAL

Because of the dangers of flying in a war zone, most flights from CONUS (USA) landed under the cover of darkness. This provided a certain margin of safety. The airliners, under charter to the military remained on the ground as briefly as possible due to the high insurance costs and increased the odds of being destroyed by an enemy mortar round.

Our airplane taxied to an area near the terminal, and as soon as the metal stair-steps touched the ground, two heavily armed soldiers boarded the plane yelling instructions. This was our introduction to Vietnam before we even set foot on the soil and sand of the Cam Ranh Air Base. After receiving our instructions, we deplaned rapidly, though awkwardly, wearing our Class A uniforms, hats, and high heeled shoes. As we formed a line, we passed by another line of happy soldiers, anxiously waiting to board this same plane, affectionately and reverently called "THE FREEDOM BIRD", for their long-awaited flight home.

The Chief Nurse and one Corpsman came to meet the plane and escorted us to the terminal to claim our baggage. This terminal was one of the largest military aerial ports in the World. It handled approximately 8,000 aircraft take-offs and landings, 40,000 tons of cargo, and 130,000 passengers monthly. It was an important part on an aerial delivery and mobility section which supported parachute supply drops and the movement of thousands of soldiers throughout Vietnam.

Inside Terminal

The sights, sounds, and smells of the terminal stunned our bone-weary bodies after our sleepless and exhausting 14 hour flight. Scattered around the terminal were GIs in fatigues and battle gear waiting to be flown to battle areas. Vietnamese women and children were squatting on the floor with their soldier-husbands awaiting flights. The unfamiliar sound of the strident, unmelodious and discordant Vietnamese language, the reeking stench of cooking Nuoc

Nam (Fish Sauce) and the aroma of Vietnamese food all mingled to give us a pungent portent of the experiences we would encounter during the next 12 months.

The GIs had a nickname for the airlines and planes which flew "in country" ie within the confines of the Vietnam. They called it "The Three "G" Airline…Gooks, Grunts, and Garbage."

"ChAo Anh"…Welcome to Vietnam.

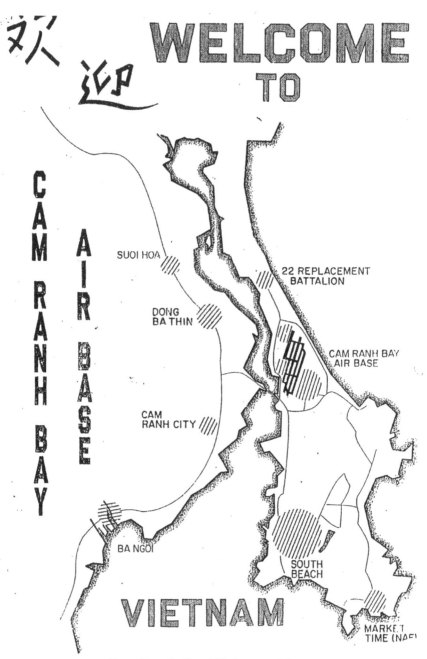

欢迎 WELCOME TO

CAM RANH BAY AIR BASE

SUOI HOA

22 REPLACEMENT BATTALION

DONG BA THIN

CAM RANH BAY AIR BASE

CAM RANH CITY

BA NGOI

SOUTH BEACH

VIETNAM

MARKET TIME (NAF)

Cam Ranh Bay Welcome Map

CAM RANH BAY

Cam Ranh Bay is a Peninsula located 175 miles northeast of Saigon, which has a sheltered deep water bay that makes it one of the finest natural harbors in the world. The harbor can be used year round because of the tropical climate.

The Peninsula is roughly nineteen miles long and up to four and one half miles wide across its broad, lower one third and one half miles wide at the middle, and only three quarters of a mile wide at the junction of its upper and middle thirds. Sand dunes ten to sixty feet high are common to the area.

The French first came to Cam Ranh Bay in 1847, but did not develop it. The Russian, Japanese and U.S. fleets visited the area but it was not until 1963 that its potential as a port and military base was exploited.

Admiral Harry D. Felt, Commander in Chief of U.S. Pacific Forces, strongly advocated the construction of the piers. He also felt Cam Ranh was a key location for any American Military commitment in the mid 1960's.

Bridge Connecting Peninsula To Mainland

Monastery In Cam Ranh Peninsula

Road Leading To Monastery

Main Gate of Cam Ranh Air Base

Steel Bridge Connecting Peninsula To The Mainland

THE GIANT VOICE

Upon arrival at Cam Ranh Base, you were immediately introduced to "THE GIANT VOICE". The Giant Voice was a loud-speaker system which dispersed information rapidly, clearly and loudly. We were briefed regarding the siren signals and action to be taken.

CONDITIONED YELLOW…One steady 3 minute blast.

ACTION…Report to your Emergency Duty Station.

CONDITION RED…One wavering 3 minute blast.

ACTION…TAKE COVER…<u>YOU ARE UNDER ATTACK</u>! When the attack was over the Giant Voice would announce:

ALL CLEAR…CONDITION WHITE.
During my tour the GIANT VOICE
is my protective shephard
It maketh me to lie down under beds and in bunkers.
It leadeth me out of the paths of harm
It restoreth my confidence, and
Diminishes my anxiety.
Thy voice and thy instructions they comfort me
You preparest a table before me…My Hail and Farewell
party is due.
Thou dost anoint my head with oil…
I've received my PCS orders
Surely THE GIANT VOICE has followed me
these 365 days

And will insure that my walk down
the path to the FREEDOM BIRD is unharmed
And I will live in peace forever more.

Giant Voice Attached To Telephone Pole

CONDITION WHITE

Tank Aside Wall

The sign on the wooden building on the Navy site said,
"Condition white".

Condition White means there is no sign of enemy
activity.

How do you explain the term
"Condition White" to the people in the van?
How do you explain the term
"Condition White" to those people
who were killed or maimed in the
building next to the Van?

How do you explain "Condition White" to families that will be receiving a telegram.

How?, Why?

AF Van Market Time

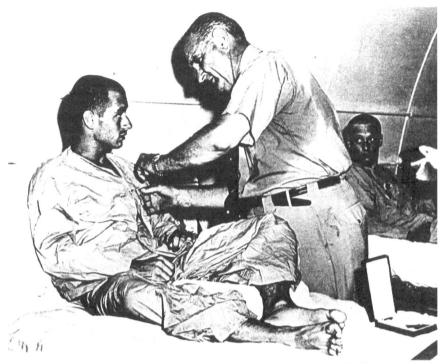

Purple Heart Medal Presented by President L. B. Johnson

Temporary Bomb Shelter – Cartoon Drawing

BASE LEGEND

*CBPO (Where you will process in)
Airman's Open Mess
Arts & Crafts Center
Bank of America
Barber Shops
Base Chaplin's Office
Base exchange
Basketball Court
Base Theater
Beaches
Boat Marina
Clothing Sales
Dining Hall #5
Dining Hall #6
Dining Hall Officers
Education Office
Gift Shop
Handball/Squash Court
Laundries (Commercial)
Library & Tape Center
Mars Station
Massage Parlor/Steambath

Miniature Golf Course
NCO Open Mess
Officer's Open Mess
Officer's Club Annex (Hilltop)
Photo Hobby Shop
Post Office
Red Cross Recreation Center (Eastside)
Red Cross Recreation Center (Westside)
R&R Information center
Snackbar (Eastside)
Snackbar (Westside)
Tennis Courts
Terminal
Theater (Hilltop)
Theater (Westside)
USAF Hospital

HOOTCHES

In October 1967, the engineers built a two story living quarters for the field grade officers. This building had a sign on front which said MANHATTEN TOWERS but it later became known as MENOPAUSE MANOR or HOT FLASH HAVEN. It had approximately sixteen private rooms and a shared bathroom between two rooms.

A few of the senior field grade officers lived in porta camps. A porta camp was one half of a trailer. It had a Pullman kitchen and private bath and a sitting room that was converted to a bed room.

The men lived in different hootches. Originally they lived in tents with six to eight cots with a table and a refrigerator. They were later moved to quarters called "SINGAPORES" with CORROGATED TIN ROOFS. The Mama-sans would come through each morning and sweep out the sand as the louvers did not keep out the sand nor the rain. Sometime, they slept with handkerchiefs over their face to prevent breathing in the sand. During the monsoon season all their clothes mildewed.

In April 1970, a major repair and rehabilitation program was started. No structural modification or alteration what-so ever was permitted. After looking at these buildings, ANY modification would have been a big improvement. The men named these buildings The Garage. The Pig Pen, and the Dog Patch.

Hospital

The senior officers lived in trailers and porta camps. These facilities had private bathrooms and Pullman kitchens. The men constructed patios and cooking facilities made from oil drums. Hootches was a slang term to describe our living quarters in Vietnam. These living quarters change several times, especially for the nurses.

When the first 16 female nurses arrived at Cam Ranh Bay they lived in tents, with four nurses to each tent. The tents became buried in sand so after several months the nurses were moved to trailers until their Quonset huts could be finished.

Our Quonset huts were referred to as "The Ghetto." The Ghetto was H-shaped with two huts joined in the middle by latrines and showers. The telephone was installed in the entrance hallway. Each room had a two tier bunk bed, a dresser and a wall locker. Everyone tried to make their room as cheerful as possible. Many nurses wrote home for curtains, bedspreads, and throw rugs in an effort to add some color and a "homey" touch.

The first item most nurses tried to get for their hootch was a stereo system with a tape player so they could copy each other's tapes. The pilots brought air conditioners from Tachikawa and Okinawa. Each of the nurses was responsible for taping their windows with masking tape to prevent the glass from shattering during mortar attacks. Sandbags were filled and stacked to about waist-level along the outside walls of the hootch.

VIETNAM 1965-1972

Even with the nurses working on different shifts, the latrine and shower facilities were woefully inadequate! There seldom was enough hot water and there's nothing worse than to be in the shower with your hair full of shampoo when a mortar hits and you stand there without water or lights. To compound the situation, the Vietnamese would come in and steal your clothes while you were showering! The showers had cockroaches and spiders but you just chalked all those things up to "Life on the Dunes".

Nurses Tent Hootches

View from Nurses Hootches

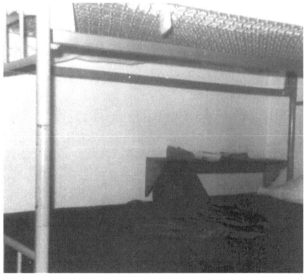

Nurses Hootches (Ghetto)

Lt. Col. Phyllis Gates

Nurses Ghetto Quarters

5 o'clock Traffic

Menopause Manor

Ghetto Sand Bagged

Chief Nurses Quarters

Laundry Racks

Men's Hootches

COMMANDER'S POLICY ON HOOTCH REPAIR AND REHABILITATION AND REPAIR OF REVETMENTS:

As a part of a larger effort to improve the billeting and recreational facilities of all personnel assigned to CRBAB, on 1 April 1969 a major repair and rehabilitation project of airmen hootches on the east side of CRBAB was initiated. Concurrently, a program was initiated to repair revetments around all buildings in which personnel live or in which large numbers of personnel congregate on the east side of CRBAB and on "HerkyHill." The NCO/Airmen Advisory Council developed the standardized designs which are being followed. It is planned to repair all airmen hootches assigned to individual units, (i.e.) squadrons and detachments on the unit basis. Three unit billeting areas in which hootch repair and rehabilitation has been started are those of the 483rd Hospital, Security Police and CAMS.

Once a hootch has been repaired, no structural modification (or alteration) whatsoever of the hootch is permitted without first obtaining the written approval of the Base Civil Engineer and the Base commander. If any structural modification (or alterations) are made without first receiving the required written approval the personnel involved will be held pecuniary responsible under AFM 177-11 and in addition disciplinary action will be taken under Articles 90 and 108, UCMJ.

The rehabilitation of the grounds around the repaired hootches, to include removing the sand immediately around the buildings to a depth of approximately twelve inches below floor level (to permit free air circulation, prevent rot, and eliminate vermin) and maintaining this condition is the responsibility of the units assigned the hootches.

COMMANDER'S POLICY

Similarly, the level of grounds and replanting around those two-story barrack which have had the revetments repaired is the responsibility of the unit assigned the barracks. To prevent rot and eliminate vermin in the two-story barracks, the sand immediately adjacent to the buildings must be removed from contact with wood. This is a continuing responsibility of the unit assigned to the barracks.

Goldie Ladner on Cam Ranh Cadillac

THE BASE CHAPEL

The base chapel was dedicated at about 1630 hours on 24 December 1965. It was built by the personnel that were assigned to Cam Ranh Base.

The Chapel was further decorated in 1966 by a picture of CHRIST that was pasted on plywood and placed behind the altar. By 1970, the base chapel offered Protestant, Catholic, Jewish, and Seventh Day Adventist services. In addition to the regular services the chapel offered Bible study, marriage seminars, confession, and communion.

One of the chaplains' written messages in the base newspaper was as follows… "During this Lenten Season of 1972, we must cope with the evil that abounds. Evils such as alcoholism, drugs, violent tempers, and sexual abandon prevail especially in Nam. We have all been damaged by them, especially here in Nam."

On February 4, 1972 the newspaper CARIBOU CLARION announced that all services would cease at the Westside Chapel. Service would now be held at the Eastside Chapel. The Westside Chapel was released to the civil Engineer's for dismantling and shipping to another country.

The Chapel played a vital part in helping people cope with problems and provided spiritual support during their tour of duty

Base Chapel

Multi Denominational Chapel

THE SIXTH CONVALESCENT CENTER

The 6th Convalescent Center was located at Cam Ranh Bay and was constructed in 1965; it was located near the 12th Air Force Hospital. The center could be expanded to 2,000 beds. Patients commonly referred to the center as the "6th Concentration Camp."

The policy in Vietnam dictated that patients could only stay in an in-country hospital for 30 days. If their hospitalization exceeded 30 days, then they were to be Air-Evacuated to Japan or other hospitals out of the combat zone.

Many wounded and medically ill patients were treated at the 12th Air Force Hospital and then transferred to 6CC for further treatment and convalescence.

Each army nurse supervised a large number of patients. It was considered difficult duty because many of the patients felt they should have been sent back to the United States, "THE WORLD" and sometimes presented disciplinary problems.

TET of 1968 put a heavy burden on the 6CC. The center housed 1500 patients in various stages of recuperation. Many suffered wounds from battle; others were recuperating from hepatitis, malaria, hookworm and various tropical diseases.

The beach was the main area and source of recreation for these patients. The Red Cross also had an active recreation program for these patients.

The North Vietnamese had attacked the base frequently but the worse attack occurred in August 1969 when the VC planned and executed a sapper attack on the facility. The pictures show the extent of the heavy damage inflicted on the wards, chapel and living quarters. Many casualties resulted from this attack. The wounded were taken by ambulance and jeeps to the 12th USAF Hospital for treatment and care.

Sixth CC Officer BOQ After Attack

Chapel After Zapper Attack

Ambulance Delivering Patients

Entrance Sixth CC

ADMINISTRATION BUILDING

The administrative building was commonly known as "The super hootch". It was a two story building that contained the outpatient clinics, the emergency room and administrative offices upstairs.

PHYSICAL THERAPY, LAB, X-RAY, AND MESS HALL

A hospital is like a wheel. Each spoke is very essential to the mission of operating an efficient hospital. The lab, x-ray, physical therapy and the mess hall were faced gigantic workloads. Despite working under duress they deserved the highest praise for their accomplishments.

DENTAL CLINIC

The dental clinic was located near the orthopedic ward. They provided dental care for the personnel at Cam Ranh Bay, in addition to patients requiring emergency dental care.

When the hospital received mass casualties the dentists were assigned to help in the operating room as surgical assistants. When wounds involved mostly the mouth and surrounding structures, the dentist provided the primary care.

MEDICAL SUPPLY

The mission of medical supply was to provide equipment and all necessary instruments, medicines and supplies which go into the operation of a 675 bed hospital. The supply personnel had to anticipate the provisions required to fulfill the needs of a major combat hospital.

Administration Building

MAIL CALL

MAIL:

A. Free Mail: Military personnel in a designated combat zone or hospitalized in CONUS or overseas Facility as a result of injuries incurred while serving within the combat zone, are authorized to mail letters postage free to CONUS and all foreign countries.

B. Packages were sent as space available mail (SAM) or as PAL (Parcel Airlift Mail).

One of the most important events of the day at Cam Ranh Bay was mail call. Mail and packages were distributed at the Consolidated Mail Room. Each person was assigned a mailbox and if you had a package you picked it up at the window.

The first thing you did after arriving at Cam Ranh Bay was to notify all your friends, relatives, and acquaintances to write to:

CRB
Box #2092
APO 96326

Voice tapes were a wonderful morale booster. Mail was so very important to us and a tape seemed like a visit. Hearing the voices describe the everyday but yet so very important news of the family helped maintain a semblance of balance and sanity in that otherwise unreal world.

Care packages were sent regularly from the U.S., and contained such items as cocktail onions, olives, chocolate and vanilla pudding, hair dye and bleach, home permanents, Kool-Aid, etc. It was great fun to open and watch someone else open their care packages. Some received birthday cakes that just crumbled or cookies that smelled like mildew. New clothes, frying pans, roaster cooking pans, irons and cosmetics arrived from the Sears Catalog.

One guy received a notice from his draft board to report to an indoctrination board. Mail was a big moral builder...however late it arrived and in whatever condition.

Base Post Office

BASE EXCHANGE

New personnel received a letter from their sponsors which contained the following information: Cam Ranh Base has an exchange center with limited supplies. Like any combat area there are occasional shortages in laundry detergent, soap, starch, and other hygiene items. You should hand carry or mail cosmetics. There is also a beverage store but not a commissary. There is now a fairly complete line of Revlon products in the BX, Female clothing is not carried in the BX.

Base Exchange

When you processed in at Cam Ranh Bay you received a ration card. This card was used for beer, liquor, cigarettes, televisions, radios, and stereo equipment. This policy was established to control the black marketing in Vietnam.

Stereo equipment was the topic of conversation in the hootches. Since stereo equipment was scarce you watched closely for a shipment.

When a stereo shipment arrived, you had to be quick to grab the boxes and hold onto them until you could get some help in getting the equipment back to your hootch.

Some Korean Soldiers were even known to disconnect their own IV fluids and other tubes to get to the BX to obtain stereo equipment, they were so competitive.

ROUND EYE LOUNGE

Much of the social life at Cam Ranh Base took place in a Quonset hut that was originally named THE PRINCESS LOUNGE, but eventually was affectionately called the Round Eye Lounge. The term Round Eye is a complimentary term describing Caucasian women as opposed to the term Oriental-slant eyes. While many Vietnamese women were beautiful in their exotic way, the American females seemed to embody the girlfriend back home, wife, Mother, sister, Aunt Gussie etc. and were placed in high regard. It was not uncommon for GI's returning from the firebases or the field to say

"Gee it's good to see a round eye again."

The Round Eye Lounge evolved from the necessity for privacy and a place for nurses to relax while their room-mate slept. The combination of nurses/room-mates working different shifts and the confining proximity of sleeping quarters could test even close friendships.

Living quarters for nurses surrounded 3 sides of an H shaped courtyard with the REL[2] located at the other end. There were patio type outdoor furniture chairs and tables in the courtyard and since the REL was rather small the

---

[2] Round Eye Lounge

parties could, and did spill over into the open spaces under the stars.

Air Force pilots and transient personnel donated much of the furniture, plaques, memorabilia, food, and liquor and frequently utilized much of the same. The pilots brought back air-conditioners from the Philippine Islands which were greatly appreciated.

A sense of bonding and camaraderie took place as we drank, sang songs, danced, partied and relaxed.

Friendships that began during off duty hours in the Round Eye Lounge and endured the trauma of Vietnam, flourish today.

Round Eye Lounge

Patio Outside The Round Eye Lounge

Martha Raye was a very popular movie actress that made numerous trips to Vietnam. She was held in high esteem by the troops.

HOOTCH COOKING

It didn't take us very long to tire of mess hall cooking. It was fairly easy to obtain an oil drum and cut and redesign it for grilling food, BBQ-Vietnam style! Electric skillets were ordered from mail order catalogs and were the principle method of cooking! Throwing breaker switches as the food was cooking; when that occurred you would hear these words shouted loud and clear …. "Turn off <u>ALL</u> unnecessary appliances …. Hit the breaker switch …. We've got food to cook!!!!" Senior officers had small stoves in their Pullman type kitchens. Whether visits to their quarters were based on their personality or access to their stoves became a moot point at times!!!!

In the bases the men made "Combat Coffee"

"BILLS COMBAT COFFEE"
Take a #10 coffee can and fill it with sand. Shoot some holes in the can. Next put gasoline or JP fuel over the sand and set it on fire. Take your canteen cup and fill with water and throw some coffee grounds in the water and heat over the sand. (Per Bill Price, Ginger's husband)

Another recipe was Pizza:

"PIZZA"

Take a box of K ration biscuits, take the lid off and remove the biscuits. Put the biscuits back in can. Put tomato paste and oregano seasoning on it. Put the can back in the box. Set the box on fire. In a few minutes you have "Combat Pizza."

Oil drums were used to cook one-dish meals such as ...Shrimp Gumbo. Large kettles or pots which "fell off the truck" were used to prepare this delicious cuisine. Whenever we questioned the source of the various articles, the standard reply was "it fell off the truck, Man."

"GOLDIES SHRIMP GUMBO"

- ½ Cup Crisco, tsp Worcestershire sauce
- 2 T. flour, ¼ tsp ground cloves
- 2 minced garlic cloves, ½ tsp chili powder
- 2 sliced onions, pinch dried basil
- ½ thinly sliced green pepper, 1 bay leaf
- 1 #2 can tomatoes, 1½ tbsp salt
- 1 #2 can okra drained, ¼ tsp pepper
- 16 oz. can tomato paste, 3 cups of water
- 3 beef bouillon cubes, 1½ lbs. raw shrimp
- ½ cup snipped parsley, 3 cups hot cooked rice

In a large pot melt the Crisco and stir in flour to make a roux. Cook over low heat until brown. Add garlic, onions, green pepper, cook slowly until tender. Add tomatoes and rest of ingredients except shrimp, rice and parsley. Simmer 45 min.

To serve, heat this mixture until just boiling. Add shrimp. Simmer covered 5 minutes or until shrimp are pink. Toss hot rice with parsley. Makes 8 servings.

This recipe varied frequently depending on the availability of ingredients.

BON APPETIT!!!!!!!

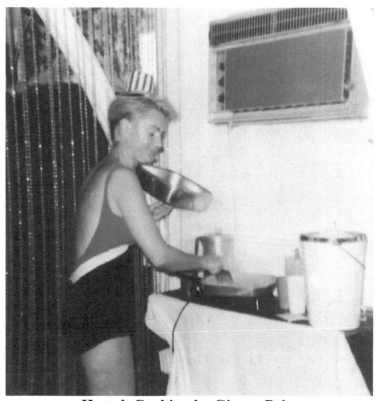

Hootch Cooking by Ginger Price

"COMBAT SPAGHETTI"

Recipe by Lt. Col. Gerri Deptula

- Cook pasta on the hot plate.
- Use the electric skillet to heat the spaghetti sauce.
- Add cans of tomatoes, water, garlic, pepper and oregano spices.
- Simmer until done.
- Pour this sauce over the pasta and sprinkle with cheese.

Lt. Col. Gerri Deptula

UNIFORM OF THE DAY OR
IT WAS A 5 UNIFORM WAR...

Nurses were notified of their impending twelve month tour of duty in Vietnam with typed Permanent Change of Orders, commonly called PCS Orders. Each person was assigned a sponsor who was already at Cam Ranh Base and wrote them with more personal information regarding their assignment. Important information regarding the availability of feminine essentials, clothes to bring, and life in general were greatly appreciated. Enclosed is information sent in 1966 to the very first "pioneer" nurses sent to Cam Ranh Bay who did not have the luxury of having a sponsor awaiting their arrival.

In 1969 PCS Orders stated Class A uniform was the uniform for travel to Vietnam. This uniform consists of jacket, knee length skirt, hosiery and high heels! Every nurse has her own horror story of arriving in that rumpled-wrinkled, uniform with edematous ankles, bone tired, walking down and stepping up steps of buses and even helicopters after a 14 hour airplane trip. We nurses said that whoever made the decision regarding that uncomfortable, ill chosen, and totally unsuitable uniform must have thought we were going to a tea party.

I arrived at Cam Ranh Bay 02 Nov 69. Nurses who preceded me were required to wear white uniforms!!!! Imagine caring for acute wounded men in a combat zone in a "white" knee length uniform. Transferring patients from bed to floor, placing mattresses over them as a protection from incoming mortars; bending, turning, wheeling, walking, running, and sometimes crawling under the bed and mattress during "incoming" required acrobatic skills. Thankfully, that order was rescinded and later we had the choice of wearing green cotton fatigues or light blue chambray blouse and slacks.

The water at Cam Ranh Base was so rusty, slimy and dirty that it was virtually impossible for white uniforms to remain white even with daily laundering, and that was the major reason for rescinding the white uniform order.

We washed our own uniforms paid our Mama-san Hootch maids to iron them. Each nurse hung her uniforms on a nail outside her door and if you hung someone else's uniform there, Mama-san would want more money!!! The nurses would later call Vietnam a "5 Uniform" war …. Class A's, Whites, Navy Blue Chambray, fatigues and a bathing suit … as at Cam Ranh Base most of us lived in a bathing suit and shorts during off duty hours.

5 Uniform War | Col. Goldie Ladner

Col. Elvira Bakken

THE PROBLEM WITH UNIFORMS

During the early part of the war new nurses arrived for duty with little knowledge of what to expect, and many procedures hadn't yet evolved. I'm told white uniforms had been required in those early days! Try to imagine what a white uniform must have looked like after caring for mutilated soldiers in blood soaked clothing! They often had to transfer patients from beds and place mattresses over them for protection against mortar fire, and they crawled under furniture when under attack. It was rough duty and it played hell with white uniforms!

By the time I was assigned to duty in Vietnam in 1969, procedures had improved sharply. The orientation program for newly assigned nurses began prior to leaving the States. A "Sponsor" in Vietnam was assigned to correspond with the initiate regarding such matters as what clothes to bring, and other helpful information. Unfortunately, our instruction was to wear a Class A uniform for the trip to Vietnam. This included jacket, knee length skirt, hosiery and high heels, all of which seemed more appropriate for a trip to a tea party than to a war zone. Thankfully, the orders were later changed to allow more sensible attire.

WEATHER

South Vietnam had a typically tropical climate of two seasons…. hot and dry, and hot and rainy. In the Southern Delta Region, the rains usually begin in late May, and continued through September. April and early May were the hottest and most humid months of the year in this region. Along the Central Coast, which included Cam Ranh Bay, the rainy season began in October and caused periodic floods throughout November and December, and continued with a drizzle from January to March. July and August were the months when heat and humidity reached their peak. In pleasant contrast, the highlands were usually cool at night regardless of the season.

Early personnel stationed at Cam Ranh Bay noticed the winds blow almost constantly off the South China Sea. Rarely did the wind die down to calm except occasionally just before dawn. The winds remained at or near ten knots. When the velocity reach 15-20 knots, or above, the environment becomes very hostile. The base takes on the appearance of a severe snowstorm with people groping through a hole of white blowing blinding sand.

Another destructive type of weather at Cam Ranh Bay was the typhoons. As you can see by the pictures, the typhoons are capable of causing extensive damage. Personnel walked to work and wore military ponchos. It rained so hard, that you would still get wet up to your thighs...I do believe it rained sideways and straight up! Your shoes mildewed, your purse rotted, and your hair drooped! It was necessary to keep a light bulb burning in your closet to keep down the mildew problem.

Flooding Road From The Typhoon

Damage to the Base From The Typhoon

FUNNY MONEY

All personnel were paid once a month by a Military Payment Certificate ("MPC") check. Most of us had our checks sent directly to the bank of our choice. The Bank of America had a branch at Cam Ranh Base offering a free checking account which paid interest on accounts of at least $100 balance. You cashed your check converting it to Military Payment Certificates available in $.05, $.10, $.25, $.50, $1.00, $5.00, $10.00 and $20.00 denominations. MPC was the medium of exchange in all U.S. Government activities and was not to be used on the local economy or for payment to local nationals.

To pay our Mama-sans, we converted our MPC to Piasters which we referred to as "P". In 1970, the rate was 118 Piasters to one MPC dollar. Civilian workers frequently obtained a better rate of exchange in foreign countries such as Hong Kong, Singapore, and Korea. We also called "P", funny money…rightly equating it with Monopoly Money.

Conversion Day was better known as "C day". At unannounced intervals, the Giant Voice would announce "This is C Day". Vietnamese's Nationals would be peering through the fence shouting "Hey, Number One GI…Number One GI, change my money????". They had

MPC which would be worthless after that day and wanted to exchange it for new money.

So essentially our billfolds looked like a foreign bank. They contained MPC, Piaster, and other currency from R&R trips. This money could be from Okinawa, Taiwan, Japan, Thailand, Hong Kong, Singapore, Philippines, Australia or Korea.

MPC Scrip

Military Bank

WHAT'S A GAL TO DO ABOUT HER HAIR?

My hair is a mess!! What does a lady do when there's no beauty shop, no mousse, no home permanents, no curlers, no Clairol rinse, no bleach, no shampoos or conditioners, no curling iron, no *anything*?? Well, what did you expect, an Elizabeth Arden's Red Door Salon?? Hell, no, there's a war goin' on!

Yet, get not discouraged; we do have Vietnamese "Beauty operators"! Never mind when she drops the comb, picks it up, spits on it to clean it, and continues combing your hair. And don't be so picky, just because you go in looking like a movie star and come out looking like Gravel Gertie!

Ah, but one bright day a miracle arrived in the form of a U.S. sailor who had completed half of a six-month beautification school! The nurses were ecstatic. Although hair and beauty products were scarce, he was quite adept at finding or creating enough to keep us going. He even had his mother send supplies from home, and friends returning to the States were given shopping lists of things to send back to us. Our sailor beautician became a dear friend and trusted confidant to many of them, and he was especially appreciated when he'd do the hair of a nurse about to leave for home.

Combat Beauty Shop

ALPHA--THE BEGINNING

The major expansion of facilities on the Cam Ranh Peninsula began in June of 1965 with the cooperative efforts of the 35th Army Engineers Construction Group and the Civilian Construction Company of Raymond Morrison Knudson...commonly called RMK.

One single pier had been constructed in 1963. As American commitment deepened and requirement for supplies, personnel and equipment increased, it became necessary to enlarge the port. Five more piers were added that were capable of off loading 4000 tons of cargo per day.

The hostile environment, of shifting sand, heat, insects, humidity, lack of fresh water, along with a labor shortage, presented a formidable challenge to the engineers. A large portion of this construction was performed by the South Vietnamese war widows who came to be known as "Little Tiger Ladies." They often weighed less than 100 pounds and were less than 5 feet in stature, but proved equal to almost every construction task they undertook.

A 10,000 foot cement runway and equally long aluminum mat runway were constructed with Air Force operations beginning in August 1965. By this time, support facilities of a small city were either finished or in the process of completion. By November 1965, 2000, persons were stationed at Cam Ranh Base with ten percent living in Quonset huts and the remainder living in tents.

The base contained a milk recombing plant built by Meadowgold Dairies, laundry facilities, a cold storage area, oxygen and acetylene plant, a 2000 bed Army Hospital (6th Convalescent Center commonly called 6CC), and a power system built by Vinnell Corporation that included five Navy T-2 power barges each supplying 25,000 kilowatts and eight land-based generators providing 1,100 kilowatts a piece.

On October 20th, 1965 the first of several squadrons arrived and the runway became operational. The Navy developed a base to support its coast-watching operations code named "Market Time". A large naval air facility and communications center was also operated by the Navy. In addition to the 6CC the Army manned a replacement center, an airfield, and cantonment area.

Air Force facilities providing medical treatment grew from a 10 bed tent dispensary in 1966 to a 485 bed hospital with a 200 bed Casualty Staging Unit by 1970. The problems in the area of military public health were staggering. Safe drinking water, food sanitation, proper sewage, along with ever present shifting sand presented the biggest problems.

Bathing facilities proved interesting. One shower had to be closed due to overwhelming contamination with Shigella, Salmonella, E. coli, Staph, and Strep. The problem arose from both the laundry and the women's eating utensils being washed in the same poorly drained shower, thus creating a literal cesspool.

1.) Quoted in Richard F. Newcomb "A Pictorial History of Vietnam War", P. 139

CAM RANH BAY AIR BASE

The Air Force runway at Cam Ranh Air Base was completed by October, 1965. In November 1965, MacDill's 15th and 12th Tactical Fighter Wings deployed to Southeast Asia, Flying F-4 Phantom 11 combat operations from Can Ranh Bay, South Vietnam and Ub+on Royal Thai Air base in Thailand. The F-4 pilots, often escorting Republic F-105 Thunderchiefs ("THUDS") on hunter-killer missions. The 558th Tactical Fighter Squadron and the 557th Tactical Fighter Squadron arrived on the 17th and 18th November 1965. Effective 15 January, 1966, the unit designated Detachment 8, 38th Air Rescue was attached to Cam Ranh Air Base. The primary mission of the organization was air crew recovery. On November 2, 1965, the F4 Squadron flew their first combat mission. By 1966, the field was handling 18,000 take offs and landings per month. The 20th Helicopter Squadron arrived on 16 December, 1965 and flew combat support missions (Cargo) in CH3-C aircraft.

Cam Ranh Air Base was also headquarters for the 483rd Tactical Airlifting Wing which flew DeHavilland C-7A Caribou aircraft. The Caribou, which was turned over to the Air Force from the Army on January 1, 1967, was used to transport passengers and cargo throughout the Republic.

The 483rd Tactical Airlift Wing had C-7A Squadrons at Cam Ranh Air Base, Phu Cat and Vung Tau.

Cam Ranh Air Base was the largest military aerial port in the world with the 14th Aerial Port Squadron. It handled approximately 8,000 aircraft loading operations, 40,000 tons of cargo and 130,000 passengers MONTHLY and maintained an Aerial Delivery and Mobility Section that supported the air drops and Army movements throughout Vietnam.

The 485th Ground Electronic Engineering Installation Agency (GEEIA) Squadron at Cam Ranh Air Base was responsible for installing, replacing and removing all ground communications, radar and flight facilities equipment throughout the Republic of Vietnam.

The 50th Tactical Air Support Group at the base was responsible for providing personnel and equipment for the tactical air control system in Southeast Asia. The group supported 5 tactical support squadrons, one in each of the tactical corps zones in the Republic of Vietnam and one in Thailand. It operated an in-theater school for U.S. air/liaison officers and forward air controllers.

Cam Ranh Air Base was also the headquarters of the 21st Tactical Air Support (TASS), which flew Cessna 0-1E Bird Dog and 0-2 Super Skymaster aircraft. The 21st TASS supported all tactical air control zones in air II corps area.

Detachment 2, 834th Air Division was also located at Cam Ranh Bay.

The 12th/483rd USAF Hospital was the second largest medical facility in the Air Force with a maximum capacity of 485 beds, plus a casualty staging unit with a 200 bed capacity, for receiving and transferring patients. Virtually all medical services were available at the facility.

–Richard F. Newcomb | "A Pictorial History of the Vietnam War". Doubleday & Company, Inc. – Garden City, New York 1987

Aerial View Cam Ranh Bay – 1966

A crew chief helps guide a pilot F-4-C. at the time the F-4-C was America's fastest and highest flying all-weather fighter bomber. The top speed exceeded 1,400 MPH.

Col Thomas - 1966

Cleaning Mess Kits

Early Base Construction - 1966

Raking Sand

Burning Honey Pots – 1966

Hospital Construction

Building A Hootch

Administration And Clinics - 1966

Laundry Drying In Hootch Area

Filling Sand Bags

AGENT ORANGE, MALARIA PILLS, AND AMEBIASIS

Every war has its own peculiar set of horrors. The boys in World War One had their lungs destroyed by poison gas and the Second World War brought radiation and the horror of Napalm. Vietnam had Agent Orange! Beginning in 1962 twenty million gallons of powerful herbicides sprayed from the air over vast areas destroyed food crops, and denied protective cover to the enemy by defoliating the forests. Hundreds of thousands of Vietnamese were killed or injured and half a million children suffered birth defects. Effects persist even today among American military personnel who were exposed to the deadly chemicals.

The tropical Vietnam climate presented many additional health risks. All personnel leaving for Vietnam received a battery of immunizations including Cholera, Typhoid, Diphtheria, Pertussis, Tetanus and Yellow Fever. Then, upon arrival in Vietnam we received a gamma globulin injection (which was so painful we still remember it today).

We took two malaria pills weekly, causing a constant discomfort in the digestive system. Some of us became violently ill with Amebiasis from the dead fish heads which the Vietnamese women put into the ice machine!

As if this wasn't enough the country side was sprayed with Agent Orange. We don't know even today how many people are ill from this agent.

To make matters worse, most troops came home with "Jungle Rot" (medically) known as Trichodema Reesel). You can have it treated, but it always comes back as a reminder of your tour of duty in Viet Nam.

In World War I Nitrogen Mustard Gas was used against the U.S.; In World War II troops were radiated. In Vietnam, it was Agent Orange.

Maybe when countries decide to go to war, they should revert to tactics used during the Spanish American War- Just charge up the hill and leave chemicals out of it.

"THERE AIN'T NO BIGGIES ON THE DUNE"

The expression "There Ain't No Biggies on the Dune" is one of the first expressions I heard upon arrival. This helped when I got a phone call from the Chief Nurse to prepare a dinner for 100 people. The PACAF Chief Nurse was coming on an inspection trip, so a dinner was arranged.

I looked around to see what resources were available. The first step was to form a committee and prepare for the dinner. I notified several other nurses to be at my mandatory meeting in the Round Eye Lounge.

Jean to Minnie: We need 100 steaks. Can you get them from the Army?

Minnie to Jean: Yeah, but it will take some of those insulated boxes, boxes the blood comes in.

Jean to Andy & Ginger: We'll need a decorated cake from the Navy.

Andy & Ginger: That can be arranged.

Jean to Phyl: We'll need Beans and large rolls

Phyl to Jean: Maybe it will fall off a truck

Jean to Goldie: We'll need 100 deviled eggs

Goldie to Jean: I think we can get the eggs from the snack bar and we can devil them with mayonnaise and pepper.

Jean to all: Get the ration cards from all nurses that do not drink beer so we can lay in a supply for the party.

The party was set for a Saturday night in the area behind the Round Eye Lounge. This area had a large grill to cook steaks and beans and was used for outdoor parties.

The menu now consisted of:

- Steak
- Beans
- Rolls
- Deviled Eggs
- Cake
- Beer and Cokes.

The committee would set the table with paper plates and plastic silverware and the guests can drink out of the cans. Put a few candles on for effect and the party is on.

We arranged for a small band and put a parachute over the party area.

The sheet cake showed up courtesy of the Navy. It was white with blue decorations. It said, "Welcome to Cam Ranh Bay," courtesy of the U.S. Navy. It had a large ship on the bottom made with blue cake icing.

New people always had a problem at parties because they would cut through the paper plates and the steak juice would stain their clothes.

Start the band playing and hope we don't have a mortar attack in the middle of cooking the steaks and beans.

Like I said, "There Ain't No Biggies on the Dune."

BLOOM WHERE YOU'RE ASSIGNED
You're not on U.S. soil,
You're in Asia domain
You're here for a year
BLOOM WHERE YOU'RE ASSIGNED
Help the tendrils of your tenderness
sprout through the harsh soil
Encourage the seedlings of compassion
to push through the gritty sand.
Cultivate an attitude of tolerance to all
weed out pettiness and selfishness.
The environment is sometimes hostile
you become disillusioned and depressed.
But you do the best you can.
You're here for one year
You deal with your fear
You Bloom Where You're Assigned.
Feed the bodies with kindness
Water the spirits with love
With the hope that your efforts
will blossom into flowers of faith
And that the petals of peace
will flourish for future generations

Bloom Where You're Assigned

THE HISTORY OF THE 12ᵀᴴ/483ᴿᴰ U.S.A.F. HOSPITAL 1970

The 12th/483rd USAF Hospital had its beginning in September 1965 when it was designated the 6256th USAF Dispensary. The dispensary began as a ten bed facility consisting of two hootches and a ward tent. But in the next year, tremendous progress was made in enlarging these facilities. On 8 February, 1966, the 6256th USAF Dispensary became the 12th USAF Hospital. It had grown into a 280 bed facility by November of that year. Further growth was noted in the following year and in 1967, the hospital had 400 operating beds. The hospital continued to grow and had 475 operating beds in 1968. However, in 1969, the number of beds was reduced to its capacity of 400 beds. On 31 March, 1970, the 12th USAF Hospital was re-designated the 483rd USAF Hospital after the parent unit, the 483rd Tactical Airlift Wing.

The hospital had several important missions to accomplish, which at that time were outlined as follows: 1.) To maintain a 400 bed medical treatment facility. This facility provides medical treatment and care for inter-service personnel, ROK's, RVN's, and Vietnamese Nationals. 2.) To maintain a twelve chair dental treatment facility. This facility provides complete dental care for the same personnel as the hospital. 3.) To maintain the USAF Medical Consultation Center. This hospital provides care and consultation for all transfer patients as it is the only complete Air Force Medical Facility in the Republic of Vietnam. All major and most minor services and specialties are provided by this hospital.

These services and specialties include: General Surgery, Anesthesiology, ENT, Eye, Urology, Neurosurgery, Thoracic Surgery, Orthopedic Surgery, Dermatology,

Neurology, Mental Health, Internal Medicine, Flight Medicine, complete Laboratory Service, Radiology, and Pharmacy. 4.) To support the 26th Aero-medical Staging Flight with personnel and equipment. 5.) To act as the Vietnam area Medical Material Support Center. 6.) To provide and maintain a Medical Civic Action Program (MEDCAP), Hospital personnel travel to civilian villages, hamlets, and various outlying areas in Vietnam and provide essential medical and dental care for Vietnamese civilians who would have otherwise gone uncared for. 7.) To maintain the military Public Health Program. This program is for the care, treatment, and prevention of communicable diseases. The hospital has a highly competent staff of 467 military personnel working toward the accomplishment of these missions.

The 483rd USAF Hospital is proud to serve American and allied fighting men in Vietnam. We will also continue to aid in helping the Vietnamese people to better both themselves and their country. The year should provide many opportunities for us to serve the people in Vietnam, both civilian and military. We are looking forward to it.

483rd USAF Hospital

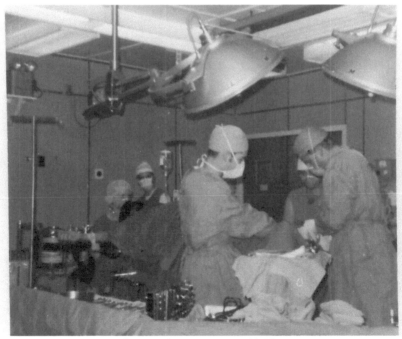

Operating Room - 1970

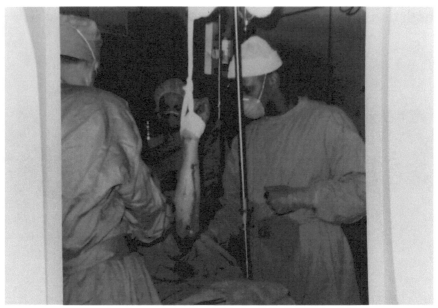

Operating Room Team

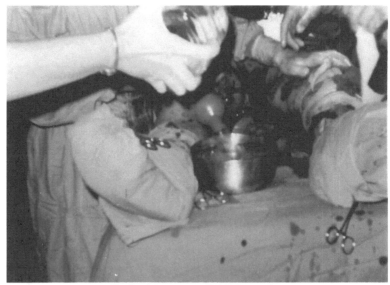

Debridement Of Wounds

"PCS NAM"

"PCS" meant "Permanent Change of Station", and these orders went out by the thousand beginning in 1965 as the dispensary at Cam Ranh Bay was expanded into a multi-service hospital. The very first female nurses to arrive at Cam Ranh were:

- Lt. Col. Ellen Respini, Chief Nurse
- Major Frances Thomas, Asst. Chief Nurse
- Elsie Armstrong, Eileen Gebhart, Connie Workman
- Dineen Wolfkill, Pat Goodman, Phyllis Gates
- Eileen Dominowski, Bridgit Casey, Bonnie Magee
- Claire O' Brien, Flo Jackson, Lee Marabito
- Cora Miyagawa, Mary Frances Gore

(Two male nurses had preceded the above: Captains Black and Larsen.)

TRIAGE

I lie in my hootch and hear the choppers
Making that noise that only they can make
As I do my fatigues and boots
I wonder…
How Many? How bad?

Then to the Triage area.
Check for weapons
Look for drugs.
But don't look into their eyes
Cause it will "getcha in your gut".
To them you say "You're gonna be OK".
To yourself you say "How long? When will it end?"
Check stumps for bleeding
Smell for pseudomonas
Check dressing, check tissue damage
How much, how recent?
Oh, God, when will it end?

Check IV's Prioritize
What color urine, how much?

What's in the colostomy bag?
What are the vital signs?
Oh, God, when will it end?

Am I getting older or are they getting younger?
Everyday that I'm here they look younger and younger.
They're kids…should be coming home from the prom
An evening of dancing…Not lying there with
Two amputated limbs, two legless legs,
Two armless arms
Oh, God, when will it end?

Triage…French for "sort out".
I triaged wounded in Vietnam
Now perhaps I can triage my life,
Sort out and heal my wounded self.
                    –By: Ginger Boyce Price…

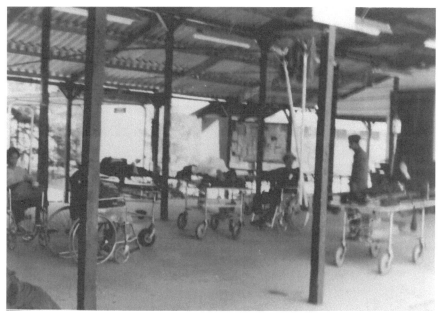

Triage

A DAY IN THE OPERATING ROOM

Wounded G.I.'s would often be rushed to the O.R. fully dressed in jungle fatigues and without time for pre-op procedures. These preparations would then have to be done right there in the operating room. Many of them were conscious and able to talk to me, and as they were transferred from the stretcher to the operating table, I tried to make them comfortable as possible. The anesthesiologist would explain to them what was to be done. When their clothes had been removed, we'd check closely for all possible wounds. While the anesthetist was preparing, I'd hold his hand to reassure him. Many of the wounded boys would try to smile and relax, with their hand in mine.

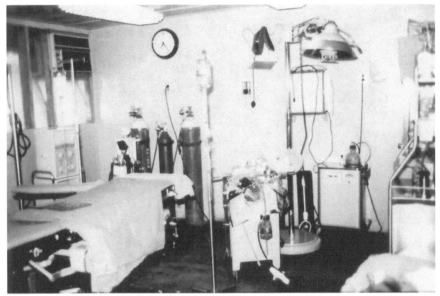

Operating Room

Meanwhile, technicians would be preparing the operating table ready for surgery. The O.R. team (nurse, technician and anesthesiologist) would coordinate their activities to keep things running smoothly. When there were extensive injuries, extra help might be needed because some surgical procedures would last several hours. If relief was unavailable, the same team would remain during the entire time.

Because my very first patient was so young, it was hard to see him suffer so terribly. I checked his chart. He had been in Vietnam only four months. He was nineteen. It was so depressing. I was moved to offer a prayer for the young boy. Finally, when the last stitch was completed and the dressing applied to his wound, the tube was removed by the anesthesiologist, he was taken to the recovery room so that the operating room could be cleaned and made ready for the next patient. It was a never ending cycle, day and night.

Please Be Quiet Sign in Vietnamese and English

I saw so many young men and boys in pain and suffering emotional trauma, but heartbreaking as it was for me, I'm glad I was there to help them. It was a truly rewarding experience proving the insanity of armed combat. It seems those who cause war don't have to fight it, and their sons often avoid the draft. Were it not so, perhaps we could all live in a more peaceful world.

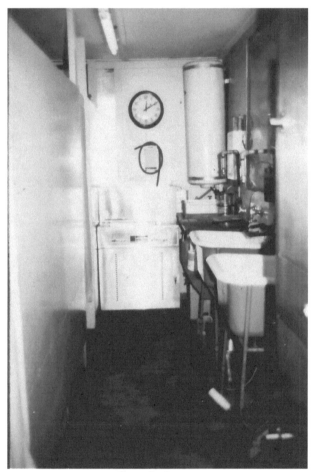

Scrub Area

Sterile Storage Room

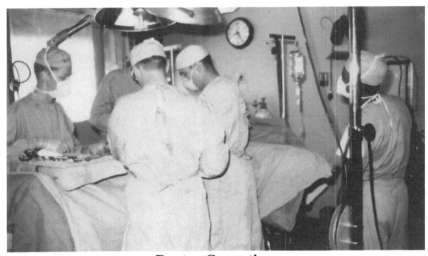

Doctor Operating

We Danced Down This Narrow Hallway Scrubbed Hands Held High

NARRATION BY BARBARA BLACK...JULY 67 TO JULY 68

Col USAF, Ret.

Aside from the horrors of the war and the wall to wall blood we often worked in, we found a sense of humor and lots of patience helped us to keep our sanity. It was easier to laugh than cry at little disasters that didn't jeopardize patient care.

Winter winds brought blowing sand and we had days of it. The back door of surgery, through which the patients entered, lacked about 2 inches of meeting the floor. Sand blew in with the door closed as well as with the arrival of patients. Patients traveled an open boardwalk from Ward to OR and so, were covered with a large plastic sheet to minimize the amount of sand brought in with them...all over them!!! The wind brought in not only sand, but also the small green lizards so plentiful at Cam Ranh Bay. Our OR Techs became so proficient at catching these creatures which often slipped into the OR that our patients were never aware of the frantic chases going on around them. Even some of the more timid Nurses who sat with their feet tucked up under them until the critters were caught didn't alert patients to something unusual happening in the

OR. There was nothing normal about Cam Ranh Base, but the OR seemed to have its own unique events.

DIARIES

—1969

In November 1968, the American people elected Richard M. Nixon as President. He would be sworn in office on January 1969 and would have to cope with the running of the Vietnam War. Nixon saw the war as a liability and felt that it was destroying the nation.

On the battle front the year 1969 started off slowly. On February 20th, the North Vietnamese launched an offensive against more than one hundred populated areas. The North Vietnamese started using guerrilla warfare. Casualty figures soared. On February 23rd 208 American troops were killed. For the first months of 1970, the war was costing 400 American lives per week. One week in March 1970 American deaths totaled 453.

The hospital at Cam Ranh Base was really taxed by the number of casualties flowing into the hospital. One C141 Air-Evac mission carried a record load of 48 litters and 32 ambulatory patients from Cam Ranh Base to Yokato. On a single day in March 1969 twelve Med-Evac missions were flown from Southeast Asia carrying a total of 711 patients. The multiplicity and seriousness of injuries put enormous demand on all the medical personnel assigned to Southeast Asia.

President Nixon appointed Henry Kissinger national Security Advisor. They hoped to withdraw the American personnel at an orderly pace seeking "peace with honor".

This was a strange war. Fighting escalated in March when "Operation Menu" began. The Americans were trying to take control of areas that were previously lost. The strategy by the Nixon regime was two-fold.

      1.) Vietnamization-turn the war over to the South Vietnamese

      2.) Withdraw American troops.

If the Americans could help the South Vietnamese control a large area then America could deal from strength instead of weakness at the Paris Peace talks. The politicians were trying to get the US out of Vietnam but the fighting continued.

In August 1969 sappers came in from the narrow part of the peninsula and attacked the "Army 6th Convalescent Center". The VC *threw satchel charges and fired at patients attempting to escape. The casualties were taken to the nearby US Air force Hospital.

In spite of all the heavy fighting including several strikes at Cam Ranh Bay, the withdrawal of combat units started in August 1969 when 25,000 troops from the 9th Infantry Division were with-drawn. In December 1969, 40,500 troops departed Vietnam.

The base at Cam Ranh Bay functioned in a dual capacity by moving US Forces in to fight the enemy and out to go home.

    1.) Pictorial History of Vietnam Richard Newcomb
       P221

    2.) ""   ""   "" P229

    3.) ""   ""   "" P232

  *Viet Cong

−1970

1970 was the era in which the base at Cam Ranh Bay reached its pinnacle. It was a small city. A great deal of building went on from 1965 to 1970.

If you give an American an oil drum, a little wood, and a can of paint and possibly a parachute he will pick a site that has the most beautiful view and make the most exquisite party area you have ever seen. Each group of personnel tried to improve their facilities and make it just a little better for those that came later. Personnel who had lived in a "tent city" in 1966 could hardly imagine that in the span of a few years city streets would exist.

Each section of the base was radically different from the other parts. The civilian men from the RMK took what was once a Japanese bunker and transformed it into a beautiful party area that would rival a Las Vegas lounge.

The navy made the most of the "Market Time" location. A small club was established that was like an "Oasis in the desert!"

Likewise the Army picked a small area near the beach and put up a refreshment bar and club. People tried to have a place to take the starkness of "The Dunes".

It never ceased to amaze me how efficiently the base functioned even with a constant turnover of personnel. The tour was for one year. Some people extended and were even on their third tour in 1970. New people received about a two day orientation to their job. They adapted quickly and the mission continued as before.

The heavy workload at the hospital continued with an average daily workload of 60 to 70 patients per nurse. The turnover was constant with beds vacated daily with patients being transferred to Japan via Air-Evac or transferred to 6CC. Some patients were discharged back to duty. We nurses felt like we never caught up with our work…we emptied the beds and they were immediately filled with new patients.

The base was under attack throughout 1970. Some nights we would "get mortared" and "receive incoming" twice during the night. Needless to say with the lack of sleep and the heavy workload, tempers flared. For some time the Viet Cong had been trying to hit the fuel depot and on 30 Aug they succeeded!!

When I think back to 1970, I realize that no one ever knew why we were there. We felt we were there to help the wounded and to help friends survive the tour.

GINGER'S DIARY

I arrived in Vietnam in 1970. Beginning the month of July I kept a diary. Here is the exact wording…

1 July 70 10:30 Sappers @ NAF (Navy Air Facility)

8 July 70 00:30 Mortars

21 July 70 01:00 Rockets on NAF side

7 Aug 70 18:00 Rockets on NAF side-by Chapel on Monastery

22:15 By Officers Quarters and flight line of AF side

11 Aug 70 06:20 Rockets into bay at NAF. NAF hit 3x…

One rocket hit 5ft. away from enlisted men's barracks. Got 3 107mm rockets. They also hit the POL (fuel) here on the AF side. 3 wounded…fires going up 300ft. into air.

Hit Navy @ 12 noon.

31 Aug 70 Trying to hit MyCah Bridge

3 Oct 70 South Beach

5 Oct 70 South Beach…10 rounds rockets.

Then for whatever reason…complacency, fright?? I did not write any date until…

1 Dec 70 7 Russian 107mm rockets hit Officers Club. NAF…3 killed, 9 wounded.

25 Feb 71 Rockets hit outside NAF

27 Feb 71 38 Cambodians wounded

12 mar 7 13 incoming hit flight line…Caribous side.

I was at NAF…went to bunker…in bunker app. 45min.

That again I quit writing dates and times of attacks on Cam Ranh Base.

Here are a few experts from my diary…

Finished clearing today…cooks tour of the hospital. I am fascinated by ward 5…Vietnamese ward. My sponsor introduced me to my Mama-san who will do my ironing for 300 P (piasters) a week. I had no starch so she gave me a can…told me when Bx gets a shipment to get over there STAT.

Dear Diary…have been in VN 3 weeks today.

Dear Diary…no date…"10th day" of NO HOT WATER.

Dear Diary…no date…went to the beach by myself today…so beautiful hard to believe that I am in a war zone…but I know I am when I look at the concertina wire…if I were ever to write a novel about Vietnam, I would begin like this…"The whitish-beige sand of the beach lay like a painter's palette as THE GREAT PAINTER picked up hues from the spectrum of the sea to paint a picture of serenity and then man framed the painting with combat-zone readiness of concertina wire."

That was the last entry in my diary…

AIR-EVAC NURSING
–Narration by Captain Peggy Moore

Prior to being assigned to the 57th AES Squadron, I was assigned to McLaughlin Air Force Base, Texas. The transition from a base hospital to an Air-Evac Squadron is considerable.

My duties with the Air-Evac Squadron began with in-processing at Clark Air Force Base in the Philippines. We received three check rides to familiarize us with the overall operations of an Air-Evac mission. On the first mission we functioned as the medication nurse. On the second mission we were shown the duties of the Medical Crew director. On the third mission we were given a check ride by an instructor and actually functioned as the medical crew director. The medical crew consisted of 2 flight nurses and 3 flight medical technicians.

The medical crew "dead headed," to Vietnam. "Dead Headed" means the airplane was empty except for the crew and the medical supplies we would need to care for the patients we would receive in Vietnam. In a Med-Evac aircraft there are seats for ambulatory patients, and litter stanchions are in place for those who are bed ridden. Every-thing possible was done to shorten our on ground time, as it is too dangerous to have the C141's on the ground any longer than necessary.

Most medical crews flew from Clark Air Force Base to Vietnam bases such as Tan Son Nhut, Cam Ranh Bay, and DaNang every three days. The medical crews' day began with a wake-up call between midnight and 2 A.M. On the Clark to Nam, then to Japan we were awakened from midnight to 2 A.M.an would arrive at Japan in the evening, making it a 12 to 16 hour day. After breakfast we reported to be briefing squadron rooms and then boarded our planes from the trip to Vietnam. After loading with wounded at the bases in Vietnam the planes were flown to Yokota, Japan. The critical patients were taken immediately to military general hospitals in Japan. The more stable patients stayed at the Casualty Staging unit at Yokota.

The medical flight crew stayed overnight at Yokota, Japan with the nurses staying at Yokota Air Force Base while the medical technicians stayed at nearby Tachikawa Air Force Base. The next day the medical crews from the previous days mission would "dead head" back to Clark Air Force Base in the Philippines thus completing the circuit.

The flight nurses were given additional assignments one of which was called Nurse of the Day. We were assigned for one week mini-tours to a major Air Force Base with a Casualty Staging Unit, CSU's or Casualty Staging Units were located at Tan Son Nhut, Cam Ranh Bay and DaNang.

Our duties during the week there started about 1 P.M. These tags gave the patients diagnosis as well as treatments and medications they would need on their flight out of the war zone. The Nurse of the Day made notations on the margins of the tag to help the medical crew, and flight nurse. They checked the lab work and made rounds on the patients to evaluate and brief them on their upcoming flight. Medication cards were made up and the medicines were placed in envelopes. The intravenous fluids were collected and evaluated to ensure an adequate supply. The IV sites were checked for leaks or infiltration. When casualties were heavy, two nurses were assigned to this duty.

The Nurse of the Day was responsible for making up the loading plan for the flight. Those patients requiring the most intensive care were placed forward in the plane closer to the seats of the Flight Crew. This information was then sent to Clark Air Base giving the configuration of the plane, number of patients, and meal requirements. Also any special medical equipment which would be needed was requested at that time.

When the Air-Evac plane and medical crews arrived at Vietnam in the early morning hours, the crews would come to the room where the Nurse of the Day would give her reports to the medical crew. While this report was in progress the Casualty Staging Unit personal were busy loading the buses with the departing patients. Above the 26th CSU at Cam Ranh there was a sign which read "WE ARE PROUD TO TREAT AND TRANSPORT THE BRAVEST MEN IN THE WORLD."

The NOD[3] accompanied these patients to the airplane and saw to it loading was as planned. She would then have a few hours off before she reported back to the CSU[4] and began the triangle of new patients who would be Air-Evac'd the next day.

"PLEASE GOD WHEN WILL THIS REVOLVING DOOR OF INJURED YOUNG AMERICANS STOP".....
AND THE WAR CONTINUED ON.

AMBUS[5] Loading Patients Into Starlifter

---

[3] Nurse of the Day
[4] Casualty Staging Unit
[5] Ambulatory Bus

Air Evac Bus Transporting Wounded to C-141

C-141 Awaiting Patients

26th Aero Medical Staging Flight

Coffins Behind Casualty Staging Area

1970 WARDS

26th AMES Casualty Staging

- 3–TRIAGE
- 4–PSYCHIATRY
- 5–VIETNAMESE-WOMEN
- 6–PHYSICAL EXAM
- 7–8 DISASTER
- 9–10 OFFICERS-UROLOGY
- 11–12 INTERNAL MEDICINE
- 13–14 ORTHO
- 15–16 GEN. SURG
- 17–SURG. SPECIALTIES
- Head, Chest, Eye, ENT
- 18–ICU

Emergency Room

Quonset Ward

WARDS 1, 2, AND 3   26TH ASF
By: Ginger Price

Cam Ranh Bay Air Base is a sprawling five miles wide and fifteen miles long military installation located on a peninsula in the Anamite Mountains of South Vietnam. In this coastline area, mountain spurs jut out to the South China Sea creating an incongruous but welcome relief from the monotonous picture of miles and miles of sand. Cam Ranh Bay itself is a peaceful harbor surrounded by magnificent beaches and sand dunes 10 to 60 feet high. Sand becomes an integral part of your life at Cam Ranh and you gradually exercise acceptance to your ambivalent feelings regarding sand.   You enjoy sun-bathing and swimming at the beautiful beaches but you detest the intrusion of sand on other spheres of your environment. The omnipresent sand gets in your eyes, in your shoes, in your camera, in your hootch, in your food, in your freshly laundered clothes and is even present on the roof over your head in the form of sand bags!

At Cam Ranh we have a saying…"And God created the heaven and the earth in 6 days and on the 7th day he said "Let us rest"…on the 7th day at Cam Ranh, we fill sand bags." It is any wonder then that Cam Ranh Air Base is nick-named "the sand dunes?" It is also called "the sand pit," "The sand and spa of the Southeast Asia," "the sandstrip," "the sand pile;" but is most frequently referred to as just "the dune."

Nursing with 26th Aero-medical Staging Flight Unit located on "the dune" has been one of the most challenging, gratifying, stimulating, frustrating, interesting, demanding, exciting, and meaningful experiences of my life. Would you like to share some of the humor along with the vexation felt by personal of the 26th? Would you have difficulty maintaining your composure when you help a GI write a letter to his parents informing them that he no longer has left arm or right leg? Would you feel a surge of satisfaction when a GI sighs, "Gee, nurse, I haven't had my back rubbed since I've been in Nam…it sure feels good.' If so visit Vietnam, come to "the dune."

The basic physical set-up of the 26th ASF* at Cam Ranh Air Base is typical of a war zone ward. It consists of three open-bay wards in individual Quonset huts with a total bed capacity of 100. Wards 1 and 2 are used daily and Ward 3 held in reserve for use as an over-flow ward or as a triage area in the event of any disaster. Staff members coming from modern and well equipped hospitals in the United States sometimes find it disconcerting to adjust to this makeshift environment; but they soon adjust and join the rest of the staff in the continuance battle to maintain cleanliness in spite of sand, dirt, cockroaches, rusty water, ants, rats, mosquitoes and other would be inhabitants. They even become acclimatized to electrical power "blackouts" and water shortages lasting from 18 to 20 hrs.

The daily bed occupancy varies from a low of 24 to the peak of 150 which occurred during the 1968 Tet Offensive, averaging 60 patients per 24 hour period. The diversified patient input encompasses patients from the 483rd USAF Hospital at Cam Ranh, the Army's 6th Convalescent center, Republic of Korea Army, Vietnamese Nationals and their dependants, Montagnards, civilian employees of the Civil service, and military of all branches of the service. It is a functioning multi-service unit. One may nurse the tubercular four year old child of a Vietnamese Nationality, American PFC with a craniotomy, and a Korean who has Vivax Malaria all in the same day. The majority of patients are wounded GI's who are flown in from field evacuation hospitals, throughout all of Vietnam or directly from the battlefield.

If patients are picked up by a helicopter directly from the field they are called "Dustoffs."

Since the 26th is a staging unit, i.e., only an overnight stay in the patient's journey, he spends relatively very little time in our wards. The patients are taken to the flight line the next morning and transferred to a C-141 Starlifter that transports them to Japan, or in some instances, to the United States. The average length of time spent here by the patients is 16 to 18 hours and this proves to be one of the biggest and sometimes frustrating challenges to our personnel. In that short interim of time we must utilize every minute, sometimes literally every SECOND, in giving total, comprehensive, patient centered care.

The staff quickly learns techniques of interspersing psychological and emotional support with actual physical nursing care. The corpsman, while changing the dressing of an amputee patient, evaluates the patient's reaction to loss of limb and then establishes inter-personal relationships with his patient. If he sees that the young GI is on the verge of tears but does not want to be seen crying, he reassures the patient that many other GI's have undergone that same frustrating feeling and quietly sets up screens around the bed giving the patient an opportunity to release his pent-up emotions in crying with dignity. If the amputee has questions regarding his rehabilitation, the corpsman and nurses answer them in a candid, factual, simple, concrete and clear-cut manner. The corpsman also encourages the patient to ventilate any apprehension or fear he may have and then gives him virile psychological and emotional support.

The nurse who is changing the eye dressings of a blind patient does not feed the patient when the chow cart arrives on the ward. Instead she describes the plate placed directly in front of the patient as resembling a large wall clock and that the potatoes are at 9 o'clock. Placing a tap-bell to the right of the plate she states she will be at the nurses station and should he need assistance just to tap the bell. When the patient taps the bell and says "Gee, nurse, the meatloaf tasted pretty good…you may take my tray now as I am finished eating", you know that this GI will soon be productive and self-sufficient individual in today's society. To see self-confidence written on his face and to hear the tone of exultation in his voice is just one of the many gratifying moments of nursing in this milieu.

In a short 18 hour time span, 26th ASF personnel TAKE THE TIME, no matter how busy they are, to try to establish rapport with the young drug addict. Many times we feel our thwarted efforts fruitless. In cases of cold-turkey withdrawal, as the patient is lying there writhing in pain with agonizing cramps again and again, we administer palliative medication…and as we do that, we let the patient know we CARE…we care for him not only as an addict but as a human being with joys, problems, sorrows, frustrations, and pain and misery. If we see a modicum of progress in one out of twenty patient then we feel that our labor has not been in vain.

Many of our patients have been in the field or fire-bases for days and days without some of the comforts of life which we take for granted. The most common remark upon arrival is something in this vein..."Geez, Joe, look...an honest-to-goodness bed...with a MATTRESS...how about that!!! Their faces are dark with beards of long-standing duration, their feet are dirty, sore, cracked, dry, scaly and sometimes bleeding, their bodies have had little if any contact with HOT water and soap and their uniforms are caked with dirt and sometimes blood stained. After each patient has been placed in a bed, then the nursing TEAM really swings into action! Each member does his or her individually assigned task and assists other members always cognizant of the team concept of nursing. One corpsman takes vital signs, an other corpsman orders diets, the shift leader and a nurse go to each bedside obtaining histories and evaluating nursing care needed, another corpsman takes the dressing cart and begins dressing changes (it is not uncommon on a very busy evening for one corpsman to spend 3 to 4 hours doing nothing but changing dressings). Another corpsman begins bi-valving casts and giving cast care, while another nurse begins ordering, pouring and giving medications (it is not unusual to mix and prepare as many as 30 IVs in an 8 hr period. One can readily see the necessity of a structured but yet FLEXIBLE organization in which coordination, cooperation, and patient channels of communication pay a vital role.

With people working under pressure attempting to get as much done as humanly possible in the seemingly never-ending race against the clock on the wall, it is inevitable that the atmosphere becomes tense and the air fraught with volatile emotions. Voices become high-pitched, tempers seethe, and the unruffled temperament seems to be tested beyond the point of endurance. It is then that a genuine and spontaneous sense of humor is the greatest asset any human being could ever have. I recall a situation in which the litter bearers and staff were transferring a heavy-set, well-built muscular GI from the litter to the bed. The patient had huge bulky dressings on both legs and was unable to assist moving without experiencing excruciating pain. The litter bearers were tired, their backs felt the strain of lifting an immobile 240 pound body, and they began harassing the staff saying, "come on, let's get a move on...are you going to take all day...our backs are hurtin'." It was then that one of the staff members said to the patient, "Bekins Moving and Storage Co...that's us...we don't do much storage, but bet we make your move better, faster, safer, quicker, and with more ease and less expense than Bekins any ole day..." and with that the staff picked up the patient and with one swift move, gently placed the patient in the bed. Despite his pain the patient let out a hearty peal of laughter and asked if he were classified as household goods or hold baggage. One of the litter bearers replied, "Depends on what kind of insurance you have...if you've got household insurance you're in like Flynn, man..."

When a part of the 26th ASF nursing staff you treat people with different ethnic origins and have an excellent opportunity to observe and study distinctive cultural traits. You nurse not only Americans, but Koreans, Vietnamese, Montgnards, Australians, Chinese, Philippines, Swedes and Norwegians as well. Each working day represents a different challenge but Saturday usually brings the most unique challenges because Saturday is "ROK DAY."

On Saturday, members of the Republic of Korea Army and Korean Marine Corps are admitted to the unit. They stay over-night and are flown on the next morning to the Phillipines. After an average 2 day stay at Clark Air Base, they are then flown to their final destination in Korea.

Kim Rabe Park, a Korean Liaison man, is our interpreter at the 26th ASF. Some of the conversations between the doctor and the Korean patient, the nurse, and Kim should probably be recorded for the sake of posterity. It is during these conversations that we Americans learn the true meaning of "patience" since we find ourselves baffled by the enigmatic Asiatic mind.

One particular Saturday as the doctor was screening patients he was undecided whether a patient should be classified as 2A, or 2B. The patient had a cast on his right leg and on his left leg was encased in huge bulky dressings. The doctor directed Kim to ask the patient if he would be able to walk in the event of an emergency. After a lengthy exchange of words between Kim and the patient, Kim informed the doctor, "Sir, he say, he say, the leg, the leg pain him much." The doctor was becoming impatient and said, Kim, I know his leg HURTS...but I MUST know if he could walk out of an airplane if it crashed into the ocean...will you find that out for me?" Again a lengthy conversation occurred between the two Koreans and then Kim turned to the doctor and said, "Sir, he said he does not know whether he could walk out of the airplane on his two legs because you see he has never been in an airplane crash in which he had to walk out...so how would he know?

Do we have problems in the 26th ASF? Certainly we do; but the problems are never so complex that the personnel working together as a team do not accept the challenge and strive for a solution.

How will we look back upon this year? Each individual member will look back in his own way and experience his own individual different emotions but we will never forget the sign that is above the entrance to the 26th ASF...that sign states, Welcome to the 26th AROMEDICAL STAGING FLIGHT, CAM RANH BAY AIR BASE, REPUBLIC OF VIETNAM...WE ARE PROUD TO TREAT AND TRANSPORT THE BRAVEST MEN IN THE WORLD...HAVE A SPEEDY RECOVERY.

WARD 4

In 1969 and 1970, Ward 4 was designated as the psychiatry wards service. It had 35 to 40 beds. If the psychiatric service needed to be expanded, as it was in late 1971 and 1972, additional Quonset huts could be added.

Cam Ranh Base was a challenge in group psychology. It was similar to being on an island. You were restricted to certain areas and not able to leave the confines except for R&R leaves or passes to Saigon.

The holidays combined with isolation produced depression and decline in morale which was even more evident when mail delivery was slow or late.

Many personnel volunteered for South East Asia to escape responsibility and frustrations with state side duty. Instead they found more restrictions and demanding jobs with additional requirements and duties and much more responsibility.

In 1965, the doctors found that 3 men per 1000 were buckling under their pressures. Medical personnel assigned to the psychiatric service were frequently placed in jeopardy. An incident occurred when I was stationed there which involved a soldier who was found wandering on the beach. He was brought to the psychiatric center for evaluation. The soldier grabbed the revolver of the Military Police and started shooting. He wounded the psychologist and a corpsman. The other corpsmen came in to help subdue the patient.

Drugs were a problem throughout the war and reached zenith portions in 1971 and 1972. Personnel were admitted for detoxification and then Air-Evac'd back to the U.S. Some soldiers even used sample from soldiers that were on drugs as a ticket for going back to the U.S. Little did they realize they would receive dishonorable discharges which could affect their lives in the future.

WARD 5
Narration by: Capt. Toni Lawrie

Ward 5 was an enigma. To the patients, it was an unending struggle with mysterious oxygen tents, tubes, thermometers, and techniques. To the staff, it was a mixture of hard work and humor. Ward 5 was the Vietnamese ward at the 12th USAF Hospital, Cam Ranh Bay, Vietnam. Vietnamese patients were admitted to this ward from such varied sources as a referring MILPHAP team (Military Provincial Hospital Assistance Program), The 12th USAF Hospital MEDCAP team (Medical Civic Action Program), or one of several local orphanages. These patients came from both inside and outside the II Corps area. Ward 5 was designated for civilian Vietnamese Nationals but it was usually filled by the civilian population with an occasional POW (Prisoner of War). It was a multi-service ward, admitting not only medical and surgical patients, but also patients with orthopedic, pediatric, obstetric, otolaryngologic, ophthalmologic problems, and a wide variety of tropical diseases.

Adapting to the work was a two-month process for most of the staff. It required learning to deal patiently with a multitude of obstacles over and above those found on a routine ward, not the least of which was the communication gap. Other problem areas were the mixed services, the cultural differences, the relatively rapid turnover of staff, the virtually unobtainable health histories on the patients, and the totally alien nature of our equipment and procedures to the patients, and the basic physical set-up of a war zone ward. This unfamiliar environment was particularly disconcerting to new staff members from well-equipped hospitals in the United States.

To further compound the problems already mentioned the age old factors of personnel, personality, and prejudice must be considered. We had to contend with them even in Vietnam. We had the medical technician who could see no future for himself in the medical field and did a perfunctory job in a correct but feeling-less way; the nurse who wanted to do "her bit" in Vietnam and found herself caring for POW's, babies and old people; and those who felt and said, "These are the same people who are killing our men. Why should I care for them?" All such types of peoples and factors came and went daily on Ward 5. They were all part of the enigma.

Upon arrival, one first tried to deal with the language problem. In the first weeks of work, one resolved to learn the language and with conscientious effort, to pick up a few words of the monosyllabic, tonal language. With luck and a good ear, one could even sound the right tone. Few Americans speak Vietnamese, but fewer still can speak any of the Montagnard dialects. In contrast, many of the patients picked up a smattering of American slang. They were anxious to prove their ability and often volunteered assistance to interpret for their fellow patients who were less talented. Occasionally, a prolonged discourse between these two groups ensued after a question like, "Where is your pain? The answer would come back, an emphatic, "YES"! Most of what transpired during these nebulous discussions will forever remain a mystery.

During the day, the staff was augmented by three Vietnamese aides whose spoken English was sketchy but adequate for elementary translations. Evening and night personnel armed themselves with some pat Vietnamese phrases to bridge the vast communication gap which looms in the darkness. The most frequently used words in the staff's primitive vocabulary were "pain, water, little, much, go, come, urinate and defecate." Americans usually pronounce words without the tonal inflections which make them unintelligible to the native speaker.

Ward 5 was an open-bay type of ward in a Quonset hut like some of the other wards at Cam Ranh Bay. The bed capacity was thirty-three with a typical census of thirty-three plus any number of "boarders" constituted by relatives of the patient who took up residence of sorts anywhere in the vicinity of his bed. Usually there were many very sick patients on the ward, perhaps due to the fact that they waited so long before seeking assistance other than the local village medicine man. Since there were no individual "privacy" curtains on the ward, portable screens were used for procedures, requiring privacy. They appeared so unusual and intriguing that, within seconds after they were erected, most of the ambulatory population of the ward and all the "boarders" could be counted upon to be looking under, around and through the screen. A similar phenomenon could be observed each morning in the "one-seated" Latrine and washroom allocated to the female segment of Ward 5. Americans with their notions of privacy are sometimes baffled by the affability of a dozen Vietnamese women squatting, patiently awaiting their turn at the commode and sink in the small room.

It was not uncommon to see "the blind leading the blind" on the ward, because eye diseases in common in rural Vietnam. Patients with cataracts or recent cataract extractions generally could be seen leading one another to the latrine, or just to the other end of the ward for chat over betel nut with someone who is bedfast. It was not uncommon to witness the surprised delight of a patient whose sight had been surgically restored. The staff expected success – they didn't.

The humor? It lies in many things. Who, for instance could have guessed that some of the mothers would put chocolate milk in the baby bottles merely because it was available? How could they have anticipated the multitude of rainbow stools which followed? And, why shouldn't the patient chill apples and oranges in the ice containers on the baby's crop tent? Americans are said to be pragmatic, so why do we become rattled if the patients shows a little of the same spirit simply because it's not done that way in the United States? Then there was the young women undergoing a twelve-hour gastric analysis with a Lavine tube inserted. No one told her not to eat oranges, so how could we account for the hyperacidity? Consider the hurried nurse who was assisting with a sterile procedure at the bedside yet conscious of the needs of several other patients and a new admission on the ward. Why did she break into mild hysterical laughter when a helpful patient picked up an instrument that had fallen on the floor and dropped it back into the only tray of its kind on the ward, thus contaminating the sterile field? The patient only wanted to help. What ALL the "boarders" can be counted upon to be looking under, around and through the screen. A similar phenomenon can be observed each morning in the "one-seater" latrine and wash-room allocated to the female segment of Ward 5. Americans with their notion of privacy are sometimes baffled by the affability of a dozen Vietnamese women squatting, patiently awaiting their turn at the commode and sink in the small room.

It is not uncommon to see "the blind leading the blind" on the ward, because eye disease is common in rural Vietnam. Patients with cataracts or recent cataract extractions generally be seen leading one another to the latrine, or just to the other end of the ward for a chat over a betel nuts with someone who is bedfast. It is not uncommon to witness the surprised delight of a patient whose sight has been surgically restored. The staff expected success-they didn't.

Then there was the old man who was to produce a clean-catch urine specimen? He didn't understand the medical technician's words, but he apparently thought he understood the use of the cotton balls, soap, bottle and latrine. Surely he wondered

What joke made the medical technician return and double up with laughter after finding the man standing in the latrine, dipping with the bottle and bathing with the bottle and bathing with the soap and cotton.

The patients on Ward 5 were the staff's reason for being here. They came not knowing what to expect and they received the unexpected. Many diagnoses passed through the portals and many cures occurred that never were possible before. The enigma persists, but somehow through the silent language of the man communicating with his neighbor, hearts and minds were won. A mutual respected arose from the dichotomy of people; tolerance replaced irrigation, fear gave way to understanding, laughter rang out with (none at) the foreigner, and good will and health became apparent where once there was none. It was not always so, but it happened often enough on Ward 5 to make it all seem worthwhile. Hearts and minds were being won.

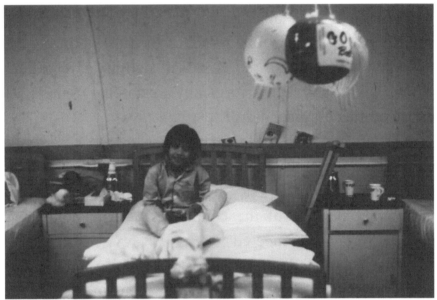

Vietnamese Patient Wards

WARD 6

Ward 6 was used for physical examination. All the instruments and supplies used to perform these physicals were set up in this hut.

It was rumored that Ward 6 contained all the supplies needed to process American Prisoners of War in the event they were freed. "Operation Egress" was the term used for this projected event.

WARDS 7 AND 8, DISASTER WARDS

Two Quonset huts were furnished complete with beds, chats and medical equipment to handle mass casualty situations.

It is easier to triage and treat mass casualties when they are all taken to a designated area.

On previous occasions mass casualty patients were sent to the various ward, and it became very difficult to keep track of them.

Walkie Talkies were dispersed to the Emergency room, Ward 7 and 8 the lab,

X-Ray and operating rooms.

Now casualties were taken immediately to Wards 7 and Ward 8, and if they didn't speak English we gave them an identification number, such as ARVN (Army Republic Vietnam) #1, and the date. All x-ray and lab slips said ARVN #1 and date. A physician would give the patient a triage designation. A one meant that he needed immediate surgery. The patients had intravenous fluids started, and a Foley catheter was inserted into the bladder. They were then examined for wounds. The operative areas were scrubbed and shaved preparatory to surgery.

After surgery the patients were taken to then recovery room. Critical cases were admitted to the intensive care units. Later patients were transferred to the specialty wards such as orthopedics, general surgery, or the surgical specialties wards.

WARDS 9 AND 10

Wards 9 and 10 were used for officers and urology patients. During my tour of duty we had an incident where a civilian airline hostess fell from the airliner and broke her leg. It was decided to send her to the officer's ward and put screens around her bed. She was treated and then Air-Evacuated back to the United States.

WARDS 11 AND 12 INTERNAL MEDICINE

Wards 11 and 12 had a bed capacity of approximately 67 beds and was used primarily for patients with medical (non-surgical) problems. There was a mutual agreement between the Internal medical wards, Orthopedic, and Surgical wards to accept each other's overflow.

The medical wards had a tremendous workload and were frequently full of Malaria patients, as there was a high incidence of malaria among the GI's. A soldier had to have malaria three times before he would be returned to the United States. In addition their malaria patients and all other internal medical conditions were admitted to their wards.

Quonset Orthopedic Ward

WARDS 13 AND 14 ORTHOPEDICS

Wards 13 and 14 contained 67 beds; 32 beds on 13 and 35 beds on beds on ward 14. Ward 14 contained the worst of the injured patients. The nurse's station was arranged on ward 14 to provide closer care for these patients.

The Orthopedic Corpsmen was excellent. They placed patients in traction or elevated the extremity and were allowed to suture some wounds. Their motto was,

"Elevate and Ice".

My first introduction to the health hazards in Vietnam started my first day as charge nurse of the Orthopedic Services. One of the corpsmen approached me and said "We have a problem on the ward". I asked him what the problem was and he answered

"Flying Dandruff". I learned that was the slang term for lice.

The next infections disease I encountered was the extensive problem of tuberculosis among the Vietnamese population. Patients were admitted to the orthopedic ward about noon and we immediately ordered a chest x-ray. It would be late in the day that we would get the report back. If a Vietnamese patient had tuberculosis then he would be discharge to a provincial hospital.

Problems arose when none of the patients wanted to leave the military hospital. That was understandable since they received three meals a day, daily sheet changes and comfortable beds, and excellent medical care.

On the change of shift report I told the nurse that patient x in bed 8 had tuberculosis and had to be discharge tonight, but that he didn't want to go. The Lieutenant replied "that's a common problem but I'll handle it." The next morning the patient was gone. I asked her how she managed the transfer and she replied, "I gave him a pair of shoes and a note on official paper for the transfer". I asked her "Did that work"? Her reply was "You don't want to know".

The following week one of the patients started convulsing and stopped breathing. Resuscitation techniques were unsuccessful and I later learned he died from a tropical disease.

We have certain tropical infectious disease in the United States, but nothing to compare with those encountered in Vietnam.

Wards 13 and 14

**From Left to Right:
Lt. Col. Eberhart, Dr. Rabahan and Dr. Mueller**

MOP WAX THE FLOOR, RAKE THE SAND

For this nurse the idealism and romanticism of the 365 day tour of Vietnam dissipated around the third month and misgivings regarding the war gave way to questioning, disruptive and unsettling feelings. As disillusion and disappointment grew, so did questions regarding moral dilemmas and military aspects of the war. Inversely, frustration and annoyance increased, particularly with energy involved in presenting "photo-opportunity-like" visits from VIP's and high-ranking military. Nursing care of the wound was the primary concern of the nurses and to be commanded to drivers' time, personnel, and energy in preparation for such visits angered some of the nurses.

At Cam Ranh Bay sand was the bane, the blight and the scourge, the pestilence, the torment and vexation, the plague, and the woe of every nurse. Sand invaded every aspect of our life. We draped sheets around cast and wounds to prevent contamination from the sand. Sand was in our food, our teeth, our clothes, and in our hootches.

The following excerpt describes a typical situation, with a certain degree of humor. Our preparations for a visit from a General to award some medals. Since these visits usually consumed from 5 to 15 minutes of our time, we nurses regarded them as a hindrance of our primary mission, taking care of our wounded soldiers.

Reporting for duty ……..typical day

67 patients …… 6 corpsmen

10 patients going to surgery, 15 debridements, 10 Air-Evac

The phone rings ….. "Dignitaries will arrive 1300"

Oh, RATS, I still remember Gen. SPITTEN POLISH and all the sand he trucked in during his last visit.

"Hurry up, mop and wax the floor, rake the sand"

The OR calls for first round of pre-op patients

But in the back of my mind is

"Hurry up, mop and wax the floor, rake the sand"

Suturing begins on wounded grunts that had delayed primary closure

Wet gauze has been placed over the wounds …. It's a form of wet to dry debridement. Now suturing can begin.

AFTER we, "mop and wax the floor and rake the sand"

Air-Evac calls …. "Are the DD 602's (flight Tags) ready?

"Are your 15 patients ready for transfer to CSU"? (Casualty Staging Unit)

Hurry, Bivalve the casts, prepare the meds, check IV's

Oh, my God, we're so FAR behind ……

And now GIANT VOICE announces RED ATTACK OPTION 1 …….

Put patients under the bed … put mattresses overhead on

Immobilized patients …. Please dear God … Cancel the General's visit…

So we won't have to, "mop and wax the floor and rake the sand".

WARDS 15 AND 16 – GENERAL SURGERY

Wards 15 and 16 were set up like the Orthopedic Wards and contained approximately 67 beds.

The work load on the general surgery wards was extremely heavy. The nurses and corpsmen felt like they just never had enough hours in the day to accomplish what they would have liked to do. Under these trying circumstances the staff performed admirably.

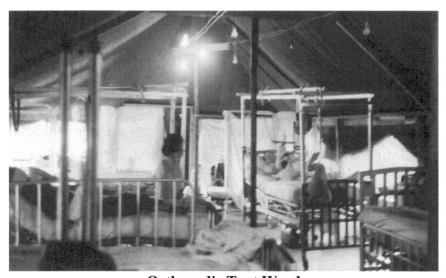

Orthopedic Tent Ward

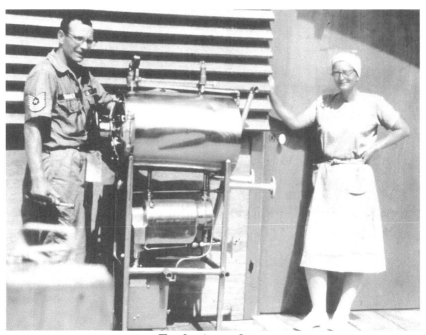

Early Autoclave

WARD 17 – SURGICAL SPECIALTIES

Ward 17 was the area where surgical specialties such as Neurosurgery, chest surgery, eye, ear, nose and throat cases were treated.

Providing nursing care to such a diverse patient population was a challenge to the Nursing staff. There nurses and Corpsmen gave outstanding care and many patients are alive today because of this superior care.

Tent Hospital

WARD 18 – INTENSIVE CARE

The intensive care unit was located near the operating room. Patients from the OR were transported to the recovery room and when their condition required very close monitoring they were placed in intensive care. The ratio between patients, nurses and corpsmen was such that patients received superior nursing care.

Developing X-Rays and Making Coffee

MORE ABOUT MEDCAP

MEDCAP (Medical Action Programs) were started in 1966 coincident with the influx of doctors, dentists, nurses and corpsmen. It was a program which provided medical care for the Vietnamese civilian workers on the base as well as the native Vietnamese villagers.

A typical MEDCAP team consisted of one or more physicians, dentists, nurses, medical and dental technicians and an interpreter who held daily sick call for Vietnamese employees on the base. In addition, daily visits were made to local villages within a 20 mile radius on a regularly scheduled basis, to provide medical care where none was available. Weekly trips by helicopter were made to more remote areas. The predominant outpatient medical problems were those of upper respiratory infections and superficial skin infections.

Complicated problems were brought back to the specialty clinics at the 12th USAF Hospital at Cam Ranh Base.

Official records show that 1,139 Vietnamese patients were admitted to the 12th Air Force Hospital between September 1967 and March 1969. The American Medical Team provided extensive medical care to the Vietnamese people from 1965-1972, treating thousands and no doubt saving countless lives.

The problems involved in providing Medical care to the Vietnamese were many. One nurse had the unfortunate experience of causing the loss of an expensive LARC! The following incident report explains how this can happen.

MAMA-SAN Sitting in Market

FROM: MEDCAP
TO: Hospital Administrator
Chief Nurse
SUBJECT:INCIDENT AT SOUI HAI (14 APR 69)
Date filed (16 Apr 69)

Due to various unforeseeable delays, the LARC (Land and River Craft) departed Cam Ranh Air Base at 1400 14 Apr 69, rather than 1330 as planned. In order to shorten the time in route, Capt. Lawrie suggested that the LARC enter the water at 22nd Replacement Depot rather than beyond Myca Village as is the normal route.

The Air Force group aboard the LARC included Dr. ****, Dr. ***, Capt. Lawrie (NC), Sgt. ***, Dental Tech., Sgt. ***, MEDCAP NCOIC, Miss ***, AIC, AIC ***, and AIC ***. There was an Army crew of three enlisted men to manage the LARC. In addition, Miss Hoa and Miss Vui, MEDCAP interpreters were aboard.

We departed Pui Hai School about 1500, the tide being low even with the "shortened" route due to the bay being at very low tide. (The LARC at one point during the journey had become "hung up" on a sand bar and had to reverse engines for several meters before it could again proceed.) In trying to beach the LARC outside of the school area, the LARC became stranded in the soft sand several yards from the shore. The driver was unable to move forward and the MEDCAP Team debarked, and instructed the LARC crew to call for another vessel while clinic was held. Eventually the radioman contacted the

22nd Transportation Btn. From which the LARC was dispatched and requested that another LARC be sent. This event coincided with the termination of the clinic, at approximately 1630. Judging that the Second LARC would be about 2 hours enroute, Capt. Lawrie requested that the radioman call his contact at 10th Transportation Btn (hereafter called "53") and requested that they inform the security police at Cam Ranh Air Base. This message was sent about three times during the next 30 minutes, confirmed by 53, but never to Cam Ranh Air Base. (At this point however, 53 did inquire as to whether or not we had the phone number of security police with us).

About 1700, we were able to flag a passing Vietnamese Patrol boat. Since we had no further reports of LARC's progress, Capt Lawrie requested that Capt. *** board the Vietnamese boat and be taken to Don Bay in order to contact the Air Force Rescue Team so that a helicopter might come in and retrieve the Air Force personnel before dark. Enroute Capt. *** met the rescue team plane and boarded it for return to Soui Hai. The second LARC pulled up behind the stranded vessel, presumable to take on the passengers. The LARC crew then discussed the situation and determined that the second LARC should try to "beach" and either push or pull the first LARC out of the sand. "Really Gun It" were the instructions of the first LARC pilot to the second. Moments later, the second LARC was stranded in the same sand on the starboard of the first.

At this time, it seemed imperative that the Air Rescue Team be contacted. The Second LARC had a good radio, in comparison to the first. The #2 LARC pilot informed 53 of the situation and that a third rescue vessel be dispatched. Fifty-three set right to work and dispatched the Third LARC. We again requested that Cam Ranh Air Base 39th APRSqn. be contacted by telephone, inform them of our situation and request a helicopter to be sent to remove our personnel before night fall. We requested further that 53 call us back. About 1745 Capt. Lawrie personally contacted 53 and repeated the message several times. 53 promised compliance. At 1800 the message was sent again, still no compliance.

By 1830, darkness was falling and it was decided that most of the personnel aboard would take shelter in the school, leaving Dr. S *** and *** on the LARCs to manage the radio. Dr. *** assumed command of the assembly and tried again several times to instruct 53 to contact CRAB and inform them of our situation. This was not done.

At approximately 1815, the 3rd LARC drew within shouting distance of the stranded crafts. They wanted at this time to try to pull the stranded LARCs out of the mud but, Capt *** (with agreement from Capt. Lawrie and Dr. ***) insisted that all non-essential personnel be removed from the area first, lest the 3rd LARC also become stranded. This was accomplished. All medical personnel were evacuated, leaving behind 4 men from the LARC crews and two security policemen who were the only personnel with weapons to guard the LARCs.

Enroute to 22nd Replmt. Depot, the 10th Transport Btn was again contacted, and upon arrival there we were met by five men (with weapons) who boarded the third LARC to return to Soui Hai. At this time Capt. *** telephoned Col. *** and informed him of what had taken place and asked that Security Police accompany the #3 LARC with weapons and flares. The police were dispatched, the lARC left without them. Our arrival at the pier of 22nd Replmt. Depot occurred just after 2000 and the call was made at that time. We then went to the SP Building at Cam Ranh Air Base and informed them of the situation. They were not cognizant.

Col. ***, Col. ***, Lt. Col. ***, and Maj *** were then notified of our situation and the episode related to them. Contact with the Security Police was kept until 2230 when two LARCs and all personnel were returned. It is my understanding at this time that the #1 LARC was left at Soui Hai that day as they were unable to move it.

As this report is filed, the reader will be aware that a Standard Operating Procedure for this sort of event is being drawn up and will be submitted to the 10th Transportation Btn. To give them clear-cut instructions as to whom they should inform in the unlikely event that this should happen again…

_____Capt. USAF NC
MEDCAP TEAM, Charge Nurse.

Larc Land and River Craft

Medcap Mission Transportation

Truck

Orphanage - Note Children's Rice Bowls

POKER CHIPS
Capt. Toni Lawrie

One of the collateral duties that came along with being MEDCAP nurse was staffing the "Clap" clinic. I suppose it was thought that we in MEDCAP would be able to identify the Vietnamese woman from whom GI's got infected just from their description. In truth, it was very difficult to track down the "Contact", especially when these women were self-employed and worked out of the streets and shops in town. We could usually track and treat the women who were employed on the base when they were infected with an STD, in fact many reported to the MEDCAP office to seek treatment. The major problem was that we were treating and retreating the GI's and the Mama-sans so often that we knew our old friend penicillin wasn't going to be effective much longer.

Pondering this predicament, I remembered the cards that the Thai girls were made to carry to be admitted to the clubs and bars around the military bases in Thailand. These cards gave some assurance that the women were free of Sexually Transmitted Diseases. Not so easily accomplished in a war zone, but worth a try. I proposed to the clinic doctor and my supervisor, that we purchase a lot of poker chips in about 6 different colors. We would then agree to screen all women working on the base. We would also make these screening clinics available to groups of Vietnamese women in the town at monthly clinics. If the women were found to be free of venereal diseases, we would issue them a supply of poker chips with numbers on them identifying the women. The color of the chips would change each month. Through whatever channels available, we would make this plan known to the GI's and encourage them to seek out women who had chips issued in the current months color. They were to collect a chip from each of the women they visited and if the contracted STD, they were to bring their chips to the clap clinic, where we could identify all possible contacts and ask them to report for an examination. If they did, we would find and treat the infected party. If they didn't, no more chips for the ladies. Pretty basic public health thinking, right?

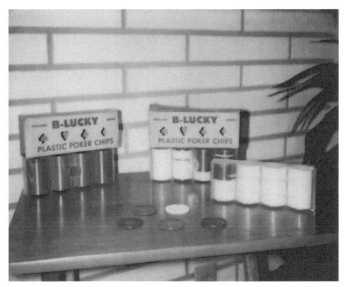

Poker Chips

WRONG! When word of the plan filtered through successively higher ranks of headquarters and finally PACAF, there was an awful ruckus. An inquiry came down through unofficial channels, "Who is the nurse at Cam Ranh Bay that is trying to run a brothel?" The idea was quickly shelved, but I never knew if it was because it was a threat to the real brothel managers, or simply a misinterpretation by the chain of command. But, at this time, I was so "short" that I didn't have time to tie my shoes, and soon boarded my Freedom Bird for the WORLD.

SUNDAY AT THE BEACH

MGIM…. My Gosh its Monday…UGH…another week of work. Start the countdown for next Sunday at the beach.

TT… Terrible Tuesday…Start search for someone going to the PI who will bring back snorkel equipment…don't want to miss seeing those beautiful tropical fish swimming around down there.

WW… Woe is Wednesday…Have Mama-san launder beach towel and bathing suit. Check suntan lotion supply. Write home for next care package to include that along with Kool-Aid, Clairol's Ash Blonde Bleach, and Toll House cookies.

TT… Tattered Thursday… Contact personnel at Navy, Seabees, and Army bases. Be selective…invite only those people who can provide trucks, steaks, booze and music.

TGIF… Thank Goodness it's Friday…Only 2 more days!

SS…. Stinkin' Saturday… Very busy day…as the day lengthened visions of the beach became ever so clear…anticipation comparable to apparitions of an oasis in the desert to a parched wanderer following 5 days of crawling in the hot baled sand of the desert.

SUNDAY… HOOOOORAYYYYY!!!!! The beach has been cleared…(hope no unexploded shells remain)…oh, what the heck don't you know there's a war going on…Time to get down there and watch the turtles, snorkel for fish, swim, play volleyball and gin rummy, drink and eat.

There was a sign on the beach saying; "Steak Cookout Tonight, Men $5.- Women free.

Sunday At The Beach

Carolyn at the Beach

154

SAND, SAND, EVERYWHERE

Sand, Sand, Sand, Sand, Everywhere, always there
Tooth-clinging sand, sheet hugging sand
Misty powdery, Sensuous, gritty, grubby yet beautiful
The nemesis of the nurses…in wounds and casts.
Sandbags, Sand dunes, Sand bars, Sand hills
Pervasive, penetrating, intruding, infiltrating.
Life at Cam Ranh Base…filtered through a prism of sand
A walled prison of shifting sand…a sand-castle
Encircled by a concertina moat. Stinging, sun blazing
Shimmering, seductive sand. A bastion of balmy sweet
blindingly beautiful beaches. Life at Cam Ranh Base
fogged and clouded by the ever present sand.
You rake it… you sweep it…it returns.
It says, "I was here long before you came and I'll be here
long after you're gone." How true, so very true.
But the sand imprinted my soul…engraved into my
memory bank…
A sleeping sentinel of kaleidoscopic memories.
castles-in-the-future sand
Watching turtles in the sand.
Volley ball playing…good times sand.
But the sand that has seared my soul is
The sorrowful sand draining the hour-glass of life
Of Spec I. Smith as he breathes his last.
In his spring-time of youth, never to see summer
Or have sons or daughters.
Sand skewing the statistics of life.

The sands of Time
The sands of Life
The sands of Death
The sands of Cam Ranh Base
Bullet Blown
Sand-filled scars of the Soul….

–Ginger Price

TAKING A BEACH BREAK
A fine sand that….
no one who lived in it,
wore out your shoes walking in it,
breathed in it, ate it, slept in it,
Fought in it, tended and treated the wounded in it
Would ever forget.

Sandy Terrain -Note Gravel

Japanese Pill Box

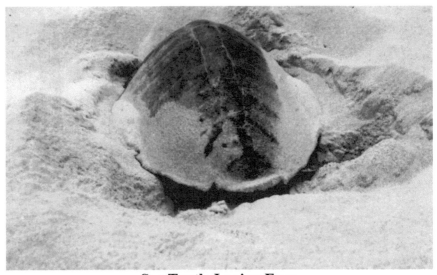

Sea Turtle Laying Eggs

Beach Closed

Wire to Keep Out Drug Dealers

R & R AND LEAVE,
REST AND RECREATION

We were authorized one 7 day leave and one 7 day R&R leave during our 12 month tour. We could apply for them after we had been "in country" six months. In 1970 authorized areas for taking leave were Okinawa, Taiwan, Japan, Thailand, Hong Kong, Singapore, Philippines, Guam, Australia, Korea and Hawaii. We caught "hops" from Cam Ranh Bay to Saigon where we boarded chartered planes for our destinations.

Hong Kong, Bangkok, and Australia were very popular places with the nurses. Upon returning we would hold a "show and tell" session wearing all our jewelry sometimes on 10 fingers and model our custom made clothing and shoes.

Australia was a very popular R&R place. In Australia the hotels required upfront payment upon registration. When questioned about this, we were told "you people from Vietnam spend all your money and are broke at the end of your R&R. This insures our receipt of the money before you leave.

BOQ Hotel In Saigon

Tan Son Nhut Airport Saigon

TEMPORARY DUTY TO SAIGON

In early 1966, the base hospital was small and when the census was low some personnel were sent TDY to Saigon.

TDY is military jargon for temporary duty to another base. Capt. Phyllis Gates was chosen to go to the Casualty Staging Area in Saigon. This was an opportunity for her to see another medical operational unit in Vietnam.

Being stationed in Saigon was very different from Cam Ranh Bay. Saigon was a large bustling city filled with not only local residents, but a lot of refugees, whereas Cam Ranh was a closed base located on a peninsula. Admission of local Vietnamese was closely monitored at Cam Ranh.

At Cam Ranh the nurses lived in tents and the patients were in tent wards. In Saigon the Air Force Nurses lived in a hotel that had sand bags about 6 feet high to protect from terrorist attacks. Nursing duties in Saigon involved preparation of patients who were transferred from the Army Hospitals and the Navy Hospitals for medical Air-Evacuation to military general hospitals in Japan or the Philippines and from there on to the United States.

The Casualty staging buildings had wooden slats and was small. One of the real shocks of the war was seeing coffins stacked in the back of the facility.

One of the highlights of Phyllis's tour in Saigon was seeing the large White Hospital Ships which were docked in Saigon.

Continental Palace Hotel Saigon

WEEKEND PASS TO SAIGON

The nurses became quit adept at catching hops to Saigon. Our social circle always included pilots who were willing and happy to give the nurses a ride. We could go down to the aerial port, sign up, say Hello to the pilots, and be airborne usually within the hour.

Landing at Tan Son Nhut Airport in Saigon, we would be bombarded by the smell, sights and sounds of Saigon. Saigon had an ambience that could and probably never will be duplicated by any city in the world. The French left their influence particularly in the areas of food and architecture. Broad tree-lined streets with entrances to French style villas provided a hint of what life must have been during the French occupation. Taking a taxi from the airport to downtown we felt like country bumpkins staring at the buildings, people and citified life.

After checking into the hotel we would choose a restaurant. BOQ I had good steaks and nice atmosphere. Many restaurants still retain French Cuisine and atmosphere. I can still taste the wonderful French Onion Soup and frog legs. French bread was sold at open air stalls and I still recall the wonderful aroma of freshly baked bread mingled with the nasal strident sound of the Vietnamese as they hawked their wares.

When in Saigon we frequently visited the USO located on Longly Street adjacent to 3rd Field Hospital. It was a wonderful place, a haven where we could purchase egg shell pictures, eat American food and relax. An artist once drew a pencil sketch of me as I was sitting in the USO. I framed that picture and treasure it dearly; I have it hanging were I can see it daily.

After a couple of days of eating, shopping, sightseeing, taking real baths in REAL bath-tubs we were ready to go back to Cam Ranh Base. Some how the expression "Everything is always greener on the other side of the fence", seemed to describe a visit to Saigon. We would meet people who said they envied our access to beautiful beaches and clean fresh air. We replied that we missed restaurants, streets, movie theaters, large markets, etc. big city attractions.

One of the highlights of a weekend in Saigon was spending an evening on the rooftop bar of the Caravelle Hotel viewing the war, watching tracers, listening to the distant crackling of muffled small arms fire and enjoying drinks served by white-shirted waiters in what we considered an elegant atmosphere.

PROSCENIA AUSTRALIA

Pty. Limited
R&R HOSPITALITY LOUNGE
29-2411

To help make sure you really enjoy your R&R in Australia, MACV Recreational Fund will pick up part of the cost of your recreational and sightseeing activities organized through its contracted agency, Proscenia. The amount of the subsidy varies, but prices current on your arrival date are:

DAY TIME Normal Price Subsidy Current Price

- Camera Cruise 6.00 | 2.00 | 4.00
- Camera Tour 3.50 | 2.00 | 1.50
- Bush Barbecue 16.00 | 5.00 | 11.00
- Mountain Country 30.00 | 5.00 | 25.00
- Deep Sea Fishing 16.50 | 5.00 | 11.50
- Ocean Sailing 17.00 | 5.00 | 12.00
- Flight-Wine Country 30.00 | 5.00 | 25.00
- Flight-See Sydney 27.00 | 5.00 | 22.00
- Scuba Diving 19.50---19.50
- Horse Riding Refer to Proscenia
- Water Skiing Hostess
- Hunting and Inland Fishing –See Hunting and fishing Brochure

NIGHT TIME

- Floating Disco Party 21.50 | 5.00 | 16.50
- Dinner and Theater 13.00 | 3.00 | 10.00
- Moonlight Horse Riding 15.00 | 5.00 | 10.00
- Wild Colonial Night 15.75 | 5.00 | 10.75

THE NIGHT THE FUEL DEPOT LIT UP THE SKY

August 30, 1970 began like every other day in Cam Ranh Bay. We had a large patient census (600 patients), which included the 483rd USAF Hospital and the Casualty Staging Unit. There was constant activity with lots of dust offs (helicopters) coming in with wounded GI's still in their uniforms.

We moved many patients from the wards to casualty staging for flights to the United States. Patients had to be constantly moved to free up beds for new patients.

It was Vi's birthday and we were planning a little party for her. We charcoaled a few steaks and gave her some gifts. The party broke up early because of the curfew.

I had just turned off the lights when I heard the "giant voice" siren signal an enemy attack. A few minutes later I realized they had hit a major target-"The fuel Depot". The roaring flames shot high in the air, causing an eerie rose colored glow.

We were all very frightened as we didn't know how many people had been hurt and how far the blaze would spread.

I remember as a child, when a chemical plant blew up and broke all the windows in our school. I was scared then but nothing to compare with the fear of being under a mortar attack with the fuel dumps blowing up! I will never forget that night, as long as I live.

Will this terror never STOP?

–J.E.

Fuel Depot

Mortar Hit Fuel Dump

Ammo Dump

Ammo Dump Hit By Mortars

A VISIT FROM THE PRESIDENT

Retired USAF Colonel Eleanor Carey has given an account of her term at Cam Ranh beginning June, 1966, which included the visit by President Lyndon Johnson.

Late in June, 1966 we flew from Hickham AFB in Hawaii, direct to Saigon. There we were rushed off the plane and taken to the personnel office where no one could give me further instructions. My orders were to proceed to Cam Ranh, but how? Suddenly, it seemed this was to be a self-help project. When I heard a rumor of a plane leaving for Cam Ranh, a group of us lined up, hoping to board. But, when the commander arrived they simply took off, leaving us stranded.

Eventually, I found a bed and a shower (no towels), and changed into more comfortable clothes. The next two days I spent in Saigon just hanging out until I found a C-130 crew who agreed to take me to Cam Ranh. Being a round-eye did have advantages, after all.

Arriving at cam Ranh late in the day, I met Lt. Col. Ellen Respini, the hospital's chief Nurse. She took me to a delightful party that evening where I met people I had known at previous assignments.

Snoopy

HOLIDAYS

The Holidays, particularly Christmas and Thanksgiving, were difficult. In 1965, when the major construction was under way the men worked all day Christmas until about 4:30 P.M. when they stopped to dedicate the base chapel.

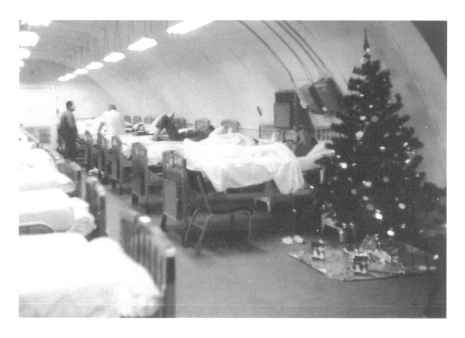

As the base grew so did the decorations that were used. The men made plywood Santa Clause Sled with Reindeers pulling the sled. The sign read USA 9,370 miles. Personnel sent home for Christmas decorations and lights.

It was difficult finding gifts to give for the holiday. We found out that the Vietnamese were making vases out of mortar shells and cigarette ashtrays. They engraved the ashtray with your rank, name, base and year you were stationed there.

Christmas 1969

When you went on R & R, you could obtain gifts but since you had to carry everything back the gifts had to be small.

The base mess hall did their best to prepare a nice meal. They had dehydrated shrimp, ham, or turkey with all the trimmings. Basically you survived because you had a network of friends that provided support. Loners didn't do well in Vietnam.

THE CALENDAR

The calendar was very important to the people stationed at Cam Ranh Base. It was the connection to the "Real World". You could check the months to see when you were eligible for R & R...known as Rest and Recuperation, Birthdays and other special occasions.

In 1966, Col. Thomas used an actual calendar to mark off the days. Later calendars were different.

One of the most popular calendars was the 90-day calendar. This was used to show you had ninety days left before you departed Vietnam...we used the expression "Going back to THE WORLD". This calendar was called "89 and wake up". The calendar had ninety areas to be colored in...very much like a paint-by-number picture. As the colors took shape you knew your time was short. That led to short-timer jokes. One popular joke was "I'm so short; I don't have time to carry on a long conversation."

There was a nice selection of calendars to choose from. The men used naked women, and some women picked male models. Pictures of animals such as Koala bears, Kangaroos, Dogs, and Horses were also popular.

Short timer bracelets were worn by some people during the last 90 days. This bracelet consisted of the blue ribbon from a Crown royal bottle of whiskey tied around a Montagnard Metal Bracelet.

89 And A Wake Up

DUSTOFFS

The sounds of dustoffs…
Approaching choppers with the
AWHOOOOM, AWWWHHHOOOM,
AAAAWWHOOOOOOM
Whirling blades in the air with fast
Clickclickclick slowing to claaackclaaackclaaaaack.
As they land…the hurried shouts of command
Soft moans, load screams, praying, crying
Fading heart beats, dropping blood pressures.
Groans of pain, tearful silence, gasping last-breaths
"Mom", "Dad", "Oh God", "get me a priest".
"Sweetheart"
"Brenda", "Honey", "Betty", "You smell so good".
"Gee, a real honest-to-goodness round Eye".
"Hold my hand". "Boom Boxes". "I'm not going to die,
am I?"
"Please don't let me die."
The sounds of fear, the sound of death.

The sights of dustoffs….
Shattered bodies, litters lined up row after row
Shrapnel cavities…hundreds of them
Dented helmets, Bandages, IV bottles, Boonie hats

Blood, Caked combat boots, Plasma bags, Vomitus,
Feces, Eyes filled with paralyzing terror, courage in their
heart and souls
Amputated legs, amputated arms, comic books,
decks of cards.
Brains, intestines, bones, slime, scabby encrusted sores,
Jungle rot, ditty bags, egg-yolk yellow olive-pit eyes in a
hepatitis yellow face.
Sand, dirt, mud, hollowed-eyed dazed blank stares.
The sight of fear, and sight of death.

The smells of dustoffs....
Burnt flesh, sweet pungency of marijuana, pseudomonas
Perfume on letters, sweat, urine, feces
Yesterdays K-rations mixed with this morning's
Jack Daniels,
Pus, Nuoc Nam, BO, halitosis.
The smell of fear, the smell of death.

The touches of dustoffs....
Whiskerless cheeks, peach fuzz on an 18 year old grunt
Warm blood trickling, spurting, drizzling, oozing,
hemorrhaging
The "give" of an elastic bandage on
a recently amputated leg
The 104 degree forehead of a malaria-ridden body
The touch of fear, the touch of death
The Sounds of War
The sights of War

The Smells of war
The Touch of War
War is so full of senseless slaughter
How many coffins are needed to bury
The memory of these senses?
Where will we bury them?
In the cemetery of life???

– Ginger Boyce Price

Dust Offs

CHOPPERS

...Memories of Choppers From A Nurse
Stationed at Cam Ranh Air Base.

Whenever I think of Vietnam
I hear the sounds of choppers...
Whirring, humming, Awhoooming, AHRump,
AHHHHHThump
Click, Click, Click, Clack, Clack, Claaack, Claaaaacking
Whooshing...like blood pulsating through arteries
Like was horses...clip clop, clip clop, clip clop.
Bearing boofies, loofies, and moofies...
Fresh fruit and flowers from Dalat...
Wounded GIs, parts and parcels of anatomy...
Roaring, relaying, fetching and carrying...
Side by side...
French bread....and the dead.

Helicopters were the work of the war. With their adaptability and capacity to transport wounded and cargo quickly they were utilized every day of the war. The Vietnamese called the Dragonflies...with their long slanting blades that were shaped like wings of a dragonfly, I can see the resemblance. Placing myself in the shoes of a young Vietnamese child who is seeing a "Dragonfly" for the first time...these words and thoughts came to me...

DRAGONFLIES

Big Dragonflies
Swoop down from the sky
Popping loud firecrackers
Have they come to take me to
The Spirit-World??
Do they come to take me to
Meet my ancestors??
But I am not ready to go…
Please come back another day.

Dragonflys

RED CROSS

When casualties arrived directly from the field via helicopters, the only thing that they had was their uniforms and whatever fit in their pockets.

The Red Cross provided comfort kits for the wounded soldiers. These kits contained a comb, razor, shaving cream, fountain pen, writing paper, and other personal items.

In addition, the Red Cross assisted the men in writing letters home and makes telephone calls whenever possible.

When the men were able, they were taken to the Red Cross area. It was nice to be away from the hospital setting for awhile where entertainment and refreshments were provided.

HAIL AND FAREWELL

Most military personnel were assigned to Vietnam for a 12 to 13 month tour. The Air Force orders were for 12 month tours of duty.

It seemed people were always either arriving or leaving Vietnam. It was almost like a revolving door.

Going away parties were always being given and the type of party varied from squadron to squadron. The Air Force officers Club had a room capable of having a sit down dinner. The cocktail hour preceded the dinner and the menu was generally the same-Steak. The departing guest of honor was usually presented a plaque with a map of Vietnam and a metal plate engraved with their rank, name, and the dates they were in-country.

Most hootches had a party area and some had local bands and decorated the area with colored lights.

Some people engaged the departing ritual of burning their uniforms. Many mixed a drink called "purple passion" which was dispensed from a large container with phallic type dispenser.

Many of the departing personnel had been drafted for two years while many nurses had joined for a three year hitch.

Whenever possible, close friends and co-workers would accompany the departing personnel to see them depart. These vary "short timers" would inevitably get to the top of the stairs and before entering the airplane turn around and holler "Goodbye Lifers".

One nurse recalls the OC (officers club) ceiling being festooned with swags of jock straps in an attempt to utilize the surplus straps which arrived when she unknowingly ordered 12 gross-12 boxes of 144 jock straps!

"SHE'S COMING HOME"

Thirty days before the nurses rotated back to the State, they would send a copy of the letter below to their friends and family. This was to warn then that they the about named individual would require a little understanding and tolerance.

ISSUED IN SOLEMN ENTREATY ON THIS DAY OF TO FAMLIY, FRIENDS, RELATIVE, AND NEIGHBORS OF:

Very soon the above named individual will once again be in your midst, dehydrated, demoralized, demobilized, decamped—to take her place once again as a human being, with freedom and justice for all, engaged in life, liberty, and somewhat belated pursuit of happiness. In making your joyous preparation to welcome her back to society you must make a few allowances for the crude environment which has been hers for the past 12 months. You must remember that she may be a little Asian, suffering from Vietnameseitis and must be handled with extreme care.

Show no alarm if she puts her clothes in the washing machine and hunts for a bucket to fill it, stores food in her closet, or scrounges everything from cookies to soap from her neighbors.

Don't be shocked if she yells "dee-dee, dinky dew, dung lai, sin loi, No. 1, No. 10, titi, boucou, V.C. and NVA.

Refuses to ridicule her when she strolls or rides her bike down the middle of the street yelling at people to get out of her way, jumps into a passing truck like a vagrant, or professionally thumbs a ride.

Be tolerant when she prefers to sleep under the bed in her fatigues, helmet, and flak jacket covered with her camouflaged poncho liner. In her first week at home be sure to leave the phone off the hook between dusk and dawn. If you don't (and the phone should ring) she will react violently--- stumbling to the phone and yelling, "call back to the other side."

Loud noises may cause her to jump under tables or behind furniture. Eventually, she will be able to regroup and realize there are no bunkers in sight. Her urge to play in traffic will be curbed in a week. She will really go insane if such words as Extend,

Indefinite Extension, OER's, or regular are mentioned in her presence. Phrases that will most likely throw her into hysteria are: twelve-hour shifts; 7 days a week; where's your cap; details; sand-bagging, inspections; mandatory parties; dirty old men, field grade officers, sand, latrine detail, and, PROJECT PRIDE.

Do not ask her if she ever did or tried to save money while in-country. This will cause a state of shock during which she may babble something about R & R, Hong Kong, Black Market, Bangkok, Japan, stereo equipment, Australia, hotel bills, and taxi fares.

Humor her if in her first week at home she asks for a pass, where the sign out book is, or if the town is off limits. Don't be surprised if she should run and hide at the first sight of a uniform. She probably thinks someone finally found out about all her unauthorized travel.

Don't snicker at her when she starts telling war stories of Phang Rang, Ban Me Thout, Da Lat, BaNgoi, Don Ba Tin, Nha Trang, Tay Hoa, and Cam Ranh. She has heard a few in her year. Don't be surprised if she asks—when's chow—and then proceeds to eat and drink anything and everything put in front of her. Be prepared to watch her place all courses of the meal on one plate and eat it all with a plastic fork.

Show no alarm if she cries with terror at the sight of ham, roast beef, chicken, peas and carrots, lima beans and Kool-Aid. Be tolerant when she picks up her soup bowl in both hands and drinks it. Most likely she will prefer to eat ice cream out of a specimen cup with a tongue blade. She will have her Mother on KP and her Father will be required to walk a post outside to give her security when she sleeps.

White porcelain is something she won't be able to accept until she has been home a minimum of 3 days. It will be best to place an "out-of-order" sign on the bathroom door and a three-pound empty coffee can under her bed.

For the first few weeks (until she's housebroken) be especially watchful when she is in the presence of men-particularly suave, debonair ones. For months she has been conditioned to phrases such as…You're the first round eye I've seen at Cam Ranh. What's a nice girl like you doing in a place like this? You remind me of my daughter-wife-mother.—You smell so good.—take off your clothes so I can talk with you. I should have joined the Air Force.—my fatigues don't have bumps in them like yours—If her stateside caller tells her that she looks nice, she will reply, "and how long have you been In-country, GI?"

If she takes hours to dress, don't despair. She has forgotten how to put on a girdle, hook nylons, walk in heels, apply makeup, and style her hair. She will have to adjust to carrying a purse. In the past year her pockets have carried enough survival gear to last her for two weeks.

She will return to you with her hair cut by the Vietnamese barber, sun roughened skin, calloused feet, a slight case of jungle rot, and a total lack of the charm and grace you once knew. Keep in mind that beneath her tanned, beaten, dusty and grimy exterior there beats a heart of gold and that is the only thing of value she has left. Treat her with kindness and an occasional tube of her favorite lipstick or just a glass of fresh milk and you will be able to rehabilitate that which is now a hollow shell of the once proud civilian that you once knew. Send no more mail to APO San Francisco 96326. Lock up your cars and get your kids off the streets. Fill the refrigerator with food and cold bam bi bam (beer), and get her civvies out of mothballs...SHE IS ON HER WAY HOME.

Freedom Bird

One of the most beautiful sights in the world,
is "Your Freedom bird". It's the magic carpet that will
carry you out of this madness.
The "Freedom Bird" is your ticket to the world.
No more will you have sand in your food, your bed,
your clothes and your hair.
No more will the "Giant voice" lead you through the day.
If you would like to take a bath, or get a "Big Mac",
or drive to the movies it's full speed ahead.
As you look back at the base, you count your blessings,
and hope that your year at Cam Ranh Bay
Made a difference…

Freedom Bird

1972 OMEGA...THE END

The year started with rumors and "short timers" anxiety about the pending base closure. The Viet Cong did not decrease the number of intensity of mortar attacks. As the base was being prepared for turnover to the Vietnamese forces, incoming mortar attacks occurred 2 to 3 times per week.

By February 1972, there would be only one squadron left at Cam Ranh. The 458th Tactical Air Lift which had been there since January 1, 1967 stood down in preparation for deactivation. The C-7 Caribous of that squadron had been there even longer as they were flown by the Army at Dong Ba Thin before being transferred to the Air Force.

The base newspaper THE CARIBOU CLARION states in the February 19, 1972 issue that many facilities will be closing on 05 March, 1972. Some of these are Ja Enterprises, Sam Woo and James S Lee tailor shops. On Mar 31st the Harky Hill Bx, the hospital barber shop and electronic repair shops will close. The only beach open for swimming and reaction would be the RMK Beach. The people at the CBPO (Consolidated Base Personnel Office) are asking people not to call regarding your status for the rollbacks. The CBPO is taking prompt action to get PACAF approval of DEROS rollbacks and port calls for surplus personnel. The head of CBPO stated "the policy is that persons declared excess with 90 days of less to go will be reassigned to the U.S." Others with more time left will go to Thailand, Korea or the Philippines.

The hospital also began to phase back with many personnel receiving cut backs in their tours and consolidation of the remaining Quonset wards. The patient census was a mixture of all services with an increase in tropical diseases such as malaria and a decrease of combat wounds. The biggest influxes of patients during this period were for drug detoxification. A Defense Department study showed 50.9% of the troops had used marijuana; 28 ½% had used heroin and 30.8% had experimented with LSD.

The base experienced many problems such as stealing, black market and drug related activities. Many people were saying they had not had any R & R since arrival in Vietnam.

Many questions were raised in THE CARIBOU CLARION ABOUT THE CLUB CALLED "My brother's Place". The newsletter stated in the dedication of the club that it was dedicated to promoting harmony among all people through lectures and discussions about race awareness and racial problems.

The accounting and finance officials announced the money conversion window at the 14th Aerial Port Terminal will be closed Feb 1972. This is due to the fact that "Freedom Birds" are no longer departing from Cam Ranh Base.

In the summer of 1972, Major Annie Lawrence was the last female nurse to leave Cam Ranh Base. Two male nurses provided nursing care during the final days and closed nursing services of the 483rd Hospital. We saw the hospital grow from a ten dispensary in late 1965 to a 675 bed hospital and Casualty Staging area.

A great deal of equipment was flown out of the base and some equipment was buried in the sand or sunk in the South China Sea. By August 1972 a picture of Cam Ranh shows it to be a deserted base. When the US left much of Cam Ranh Bay was reclaimed by ever shifting sand.

In immense complex Cam Ranh Base built at the cost of 2.2 billion dollars is today a port of call for the Soviet Navy. Due to the presence of the Soviet Navy, tourists are restricted and you never see and pictures, information, or reports in magazines or newspapers. This ended an area for "America's longest war."

1 America and Vietnam
–Albert Morrin P 227

THAT WAS A CRAZY MIXED UP WAR
1994…February 19th.

That was a crazy mixed-war…
Not at all what I thought it would be
Not like my Fathers WWI
Nor my husbands, brother or Sister-in-Laws's WWII.
It wasn't Veronica Lake in "SO PROUDLY WE HAIL"
Nor did the soldiers look or act like Jon Wayne.
Instead it was…
Body counts, MIA and KIA
Count-down calendars and wake-up days
Lifers, grunts, alcohol and drugs.
Fast promotions and slow deaths.
Napalm burns, DMZ, and no-fire zones
Double amputees, armless arms
Triple amputees, legless legs.
Quadruple amputees
The dichotomy of that war…even today blows my mind.
Humanity and brutality, compassion and cruelty.
Political infighting and professional back-stabbing
Courage and cowardice, poverty and plenty.
Flak jackets and French Bread
Pouilly Fouise in paper cups
Plastic knives and filet mignon
Sappers, Ao dais, and Saigon tea.
The horrors and honors of war
The logistics and statistics

Heart-given nursing and healing
Black-Market wheeling and dealing.
Triumph and tragedy
Bureaucratic bungling and unbelievable bravery.
It wasn't a black and white war…it became blurred.
What was right? What was wrong?
Who, where, and what was the enemy?
Was it Mama-san, Papa-san, children…were they VC????

Today I ask…
Where is the victory we won?
Where is the peace with honor?
Where is the freedom we upheld?
Where is the democracy we fought for?

Ask the dead…
Ask the 58,191 souls…
Did you receive an answer?

– Ginger Boyce Price.

Women who served in Vietnam.
Dedication of the Statue in Washington D.C. to honor women
that served during the Vietnam Era

Carolyn Eberhart and Eleanor Weatherford

EPILOGUE
"JOURNEY OF TEARS"

After the exodus of the American troops from Cam Ranh Bay, we seldom received any news about the area.

When I went to Washington for the Veterans Day Ceremonies, I spoke to several of the soldiers that have made trips back to Vietnam. These troops heard that Cam Ranh was deserted for a period of time. They said the buildings were stripped for fixtures and lumber.

The boats that were given to the Vietnamese to protect the coast were stripped of vital parts and sold in the black markets. Later the South Vietnamese used the base to house families of the troops.

The worst period was when the North Vietnamese began the offensive to take over the South Vietnamese. As the offensive started the people began the long trek from the DMZ south. In Da Nang people fought to get on overloaded boats and on airplanes that was leaving.

The march was called the "Journey of Tears." Many children and older people died on the march and in the boats. They said dead children were piled on the docks at Cam Ranh Bay.

There were approximately 35,000 refugees at the base. Water was scarce to handle that number of people so a decision was made to take them to Phan Rang, a base further south.

The stories say that the North Vietnamese were moving so fast that they overtook the people before they could get to Phan Rang.

After the war was over, the Russians demanded payment for their supplies and help. Since money was a problem, the Vietnamese could only pay by letting the Russians use Cam Ranh Bay.

The Russian quadrupled the size of the facilities. In the late 80's satellite pictures show the Russians had a large military presence in the form of ships and airplanes.

Recent articles in New York newspaper tell plans for Club Med to build a facility just north of the base on one of the beautiful beaches.

The Vietnamese have had talks with the U.S. Navy about the Americans returning to the Base.

After all the horrible fighting and destruction, I sincerely hope the Vietnamese can have peace and a chance to rebuild their beautiful country.

–J.E.

WHO'S SLEEPING IN MY HOOTCH?
Some nights in Florida when I sit
in the backyard, and and look at the
broad sky and stars and see the
palm frons; my mind
wanders back to Vietnam

My brain forms a mental picture of
the base at Cam Ranh Bay and I wonder
if I would recognize the place if I
Went back…was I REALLY There???
What happened to the terminal and all those Quonset huts?
When I read accounts of people that
have returned to Vietnam no one ever
mentions Cam Ranh Base.

Does Detroit Avenue and Palm Drive
still exist? Is the Round Eye Lounge
still there? But mainly I want to
know "Who's sleeping in my hootch"?

-Jean Eberhart

Air Force Nurse Corp Parade

ACKNOWLEDGEMENTS

I would like to acknowledge the contributions, encouragement and support of the many people who were instrumental in writing this book.

The pictures and stories for the book were collected a number of years ago. My friend, Janice Stroud Sentif, received all the material I had complied over the years and she began to work on the book. If she had only known how big of a project she had taken on! She contacted her granddaughter, Kelly Overfield, a Journalism major, and a Tampa Attorney, and together they began to make this book a reality. In addition, this book would not have been possible without the assistance of Arthur Sentif, Jan's husband, who spent countless hours processing all of the photographs and providing them many hours of moral support and Nikkie Worley, Kelly's legal assistant, who spent numerous hours typing, scanning and editing this book.

I met a nurse named Ginger Price at Cam Ranh Base, we went our separate ways, and was I unaware that both of us resided in Tampa until Jeanne Sones, manager of the Beauty Shop at MacDill, reunited us. Thanks Jeanne.

Thanks to all the Colonels, Lt. Colonels, Majors, Captains, and other military personnel who took this journey with me.

A special thanks goes to Lt. Commander Virginia Price and her late husband Bill for their support and encouragement.

I would like to thank my family and friends for their support and enthusiasm.

If I have omitted anyone it certainly was not my intent and I hope that I will be forgiven.

Made in United States
Troutdale, OR
05/15/2024